MALE UNDERACHIEVEMENT IN HIGH SCHOOL EDUCATION

MALE UNDERACHIEVEMENT IN HIGH SCHOOL EDUCATION
In Jamaica, Barbados, and St Vincent and the Grenadines

ODETTE PARRY

CENTRE FOR GENDER AND DEVELOPMENT STUDIES
Mona, Jamaica

and

Canoe Press
Barbados • Jamaica • Trinidad and Tobago

Canoe Press University of the West Indies
1A Aqueduct Flats Mona
Kingston 7 Jamaica

© 2000 by Odette Parry
All rights reserved. Published 2000

04 03 02   5 4 3 2

CATALOGUING IN PUBLICATION DATA

Parry, Odette.
Male underachievement in high school education in Jamaica, Barbados, and St Vincent and the Grenadines / Odette Parry.

p. cm.
Includes bibliographical references.

ISBN: 976-8125-073-X

1. Boys – Education – Jamaica. 2. Boys – Education – Barbados. 3. Boys – Education – St Vincent. 4. Sex differences in education – Jamaica. 5. Sex differences in education – Barbados. 6. Sex differences in education – St Vincent. 7. Underachievers – Jamaica. 8. Underachievers – Barbados. 9. Underachievers – St Vincent. I. Title.

LC1390.P38 2000   371.823

Cover and book design by Robert Harris

Printed in Canada

This publication has been funded by the Centre for Gender and Development Studies, University of the West Indies, Mona

Contents

Acknowledgements / vi

Introduction / 1

Gender and Caribbean High School Achievement / 5

The Study Methods / 8

Background to the Research / 18

Gender Expectations / 22

The Use of Verbal Discipline / 25

The Issue of Male Role Models / 31

Coeducation Versus Single Sex Schools / 35

Gender Socialization: Issues of Nature and Nurture / 40

Sex/Gender Identity Development / 46

Concluding Discussion / 54

Appendixes

Appendix 1: Policy Options and Practical Solutions / 62

Appendix 2: Summary of Research Findings / 65

Bibliography / 69

Acknowledgements

This report is based upon a research project funded jointly by the United Nations Children's Fund (UNICEF) and the Institute of Social and Economic Research (ISER, now Sir Arthur Lewis Institute of Social and Economic Studies), University of the West Indies (UWI), Jamaica. I am indebted to the agencies that allowed us access to their institutions, members and official records, including Ministries of Education in Jamaica, Barbados and St Vincent, and the Caribbean Examinations Council (CXC) in Jamaica and Barbados.

I am particularly grateful to head teachers for showing an interest in the research and allowing us into their schools. The level of interest and support shown by teachers and guidance counsellors may be measured by their willingness to invite us into their classrooms and give up valuable time to talk with us about educational issues and problems which they routinely face.

Without the cooperation of all the above-mentioned individuals plus the support of research colleagues, the two research assistants, Florence Pearson and Nicky MacDonald, and our project administrator, Judy Tavares, this research would not have been possible. I would also like to thank Dr Patricia Mohammed from the Centre for Gender and Development, UWI, for her interest and support, and Linda Speth at the UWI Press.

Introduction

The research upon which this publication is based came about because of growing regional (as well as international) concern about the educational performances of males. This concern reflects wider social anxiety about the plight of men more generally and black men in particular, and has culminated in the 'marginalized male' thesis which has gained much popular support as well as academic attention.

Among academics the concept of male marginalization has provoked a mixed response. Pedro Noguera (1996) has taken issue with the usage of terms such as 'crisis', 'at risk', 'marginal' and 'endangered' to describe the plight of black males in America, Britain and the anglophone Caribbean. While not disputing the broad array of social and economic indicators that may locate many black males in lower socioeconomic categories, black women, he argues, are rendered invisible. He asks, "What does this mean for black women and aren't they in crisis too?" Furthermore, the term 'crisis' suggests a short-term urgency brought about by recent events, whereas Noguera points out there is nothing new about the problems black men currently face and nor is there evidence that their situation is improving. On the contrary, both in America and the Caribbean available figures suggest that, first, things are worsening for black men and, second, hardships they are facing are no more than those facing black women. Noguera also points out how the construction of marginalized man makes an implicit assumption that black males share the same experiences and problems as white males and also that all black men share identical problems.

There is a valuable lesson here to be learnt from feminist research which has taught us that it is important not to make assumptions or base any analysis of Caribbean women on extrapolations from our understandings of the experiences of women elsewhere. Feminist research in both America and Britain, for example, highlights the dissimilarities between constructions of black female gender identity and mainstream white female constructions of femininity (Dill 1987; Mirza 1992), and examination of these differences has helped us to understand the unique situation which different women experience in different societies.

Building on this experience, we should stress the uniqueness of the experience of Caribbean males and critically appraise accounts of men's situation in every race, class and culture. Any more simplistic explanations would lead inevitably to the misrepresentation of Caribbean men, whose attitudes, behaviours and interpersonal relationships are arguably adaptations to a range of factors. These include structural and economic constraints, environmental factors, Caribbean images of manhood, and conflicting values and norms of wider society.

Furthermore, we must particularly avoid extrapolating our findings about white male experience, in either the Caribbean or elsewhere, to the experiences of Caribbean black men. Again, this is a point central to feminist arguments. Mirza (1992) in Britain, for example, has demonstrated that the reproduction of white gender disadvantage is inappropriate in a black context because cultural constructions of femininity among Afro-Caribbean women are fundamentally different from the forms of femininity among their white peers. For example, the black women in Mirza's study expressed an ideology that emphasized the relative autonomy of both male and female roles and which Mirza attributes to the external imposition of oppression and brutality. The young black Afro-Caribbean women in Britain whom Mirza studied had not adopted the dominant Eurocentric ideology in which gender is regarded as the basis for the opposition of roles and values. They also had different concepts of masculinity and femininity from their white peers. One striking difference was the few distinctions that the young women made between male and female abilities and attributes with regard to work and the labour market.

Sutton and Makiesky-Barrow (1977) in their classic study in Barbados suggested why this particular definition of masculinity and femininity should result in greater female participation in the labour market. They argued how distinct qualities of masculine and feminine sexual and reproductive abilities are not viewed by either sex as a basis for different male and female capacities. This is quite removed from the self-limiting and negative sexual identities Euro-American women have experienced.

While the focus of this feminist work has been on women, it has clear implications for the study of men and does highlight the importance of reaching a cultural understanding of gender dynamics, rather than studying men in isolation. For this reason, the study of male educational performance presented here does not rest solely on an account of male educational experience.

Reaching cultural understandings of any behaviour has implications both for how the research is carried out and also for the appropriateness of those engaged to do so. While issues relating to choice of methods are elaborated later, here I would like to briefly turn to those involved in the study. The research was designed by myself with assistance from colleagues at the University of the West Indies (UWI). Data were collected by myself in all schools that took part in the study along with research assistance in Jamaica and Barbados. In Jamaica, Florence Pearson worked as research assistant doing observation and interviewing alongside me in schools; and in Barbados I was assisted by Nicky MacDonald. As researchers we came from different cultural backgrounds than each other and also from those who participated in the research. Here we acknowledge these differences and the implications that they may have for this account of the research.

Both Florence and Nicky brought quite different interests and experiences to the project. Florence is a black Jamaican female and the cultural and gender-specific experiences she brought to the project were very important. She was able to develop more spontaneous and easier relationships with the respondents with whom she shared a range of cultural understandings. It was apparent that some respondents talked to Florence in a way they could not talk to me as a white European female outsider. At the same time, there were conversations that occurred between myself and respondents which happened precisely because I was seen as different, foreign and 'temporary'. These characteristics made me less 'threatening' or 'important', and hence topics were raised which would have seemed dangerous to share with a Jamaican researcher. In Barbados, Nicky, a white Canadian woman, carried out observation and interviewing alongside me in schools. Nicky is an experienced teacher, having taught in Canada and the West Indies, and this experience was an enormous asset to the research. Drawing on her teaching experiences, she was able to develop very good rapport with teachers who took part. Furthermore, her knowledge of curriculum and pedagogy informed our discussions, the issues that were raised and the analysis of data that we collected. I also found that similar to the experience in Jamaica, there were some topics that participants felt happier to discuss with Nicky and some with me. While some teachers were clearly pleased to be interviewed by a teacher who understood teaching, others found it threatening and were wary of implied criticism of the methods they used.

The relationship between respondent and researcher is central to the methodology with which the study most identified. This was a qualitative study that relied primarily upon in-depth interviewing and participant observation. Whereas quantitative (positivistic) methodologies claim that objects of study exist independently from both the agents and tools of research, qualitative methodologies are based upon the premise that data does not exist independently but is constructed through the process of research and through the relationship between researcher and respondent. This is a fundamental tenet of feminist methods that take issue with the mythology of what Oakley (1981) describes as 'hygiene' research, in which the role of the researcher is treated as both neutral and invisible. In rejecting this approach feminist researchers suggest personal involvement must be "the condition under which people come to know each other and to admit others into their lives" (Oakley 1981). While the cultural differences and varied experiences we brought with us to the study undoubtedly did have implications for the extent to which we could know the respondents, we tried to address this through our concerted efforts to understand their experiences within the wider context (social and historical) of their lives.

Gender and Caribbean High School Achievement

Levels of educational attainment have been a focus of concern in the Caribbean, and as a result school underachievement has been explored in relation to a range of variables. A recurring theme in the educational research literature highlights the different levels of achievement for males and females in Caribbean systems of education. Research approaches to gender-differentiated performance have focused on several areas. These include demographic variables and home background (Gordon 1989), biological differences (Miller 1986) and gender aptitudes (Cuffie 1989), school organization (Leo-Rhynie 1989; Salter 1989), curriculum and pedagogy (Ayodike 1989; Watts 1989; Drayton 1991) the gender ratio of teachers (Miller 1991; Leo-Rhynie 1989; Schiefelbein and Peruzzi 1991), expectations of teachers and pupils (Payne 1988; Salter 1989; Hamilton 1981) and pupil subcultures (Leo-Rhynie 1989, 1992).

Most recent concern with gender-differentiated achievement in the Caribbean reflects a global concern about the underperformance of males. Whilst the school experience of males has been far from invisible in the research literature (until recently the relationship between social class and educational mobility was measured exclusively in terms of male experiences), issues in gender performance explored by recent researchers have primarily focused upon females.

In the developed world, recent research shows that, whilst the domains of academic achievement continue to differ by gender, the popular stereotype of the female underachiever is now largely unfounded (Stockard and Wood 1984; Klein 1985). It appears rather that women are motivated to achieve equally or surpass men in educational attainment (Klein 1985; Stockard 1985; Stockard and Wood 1984; Mickelson 1992) and this is despite unequal opportunities that they face in the occupational structure upon leaving school (Mickelson 1992). At the same time, however, the best paying careers usually require strong background in math and science and women lag behind men in these areas (Stockard

1985). Furthermore, the link between schooling, work and income is divisive in that even though women have all but closed the overall gap in educational attainment between the sexes, they are not equitably rewarded for their accomplishments.

In the developing world these trends in education are equally apparent. Caribbean females are largely outperforming their male peers. Females do better than males at both primary and secondary levels of schooling (World Bank 1993). Gender differences in performance are most noticeable at the first level of testing, the Common Entrance Examination (CEE), where females achieve a higher proportion of high school places even where assessment policies have attempted to redress the gender imbalance by discriminating in favour of males.

World Bank figures show the majority of Caribbean Examinations Council (CXC) passes are claimed by females, although results indicate that subject choices follow a traditional pattern with females highly visible in arts and males in sciences (Whitely 1994). In 1993, 54.3 percent of the entries for all subjects in Jamaica were from females and 45.7 percent were males. Of the total grade one results, 36.4 percent went to males and 54.3 percent went to females. A comparison of English with physics grade results shows 81.4 percent of the grade one results taken by females and 60.7 percent of the grade one physics taken by males.

Figures available for Barbados and St Vincent show similar trends. In Barbados 59.6 percent of passes in English A went to females and 63.9 percent of the passes in biology. In physics males did marginally better than the females taking 55.5 percent of the passes. In St Vincent, 58.1 percent of English A passes went to females and 58.7 percent of passes in biology. In physics gender differences in performance were negligible with males claiming 50.7 percent of the passes. Overall in Barbados, for all subjects, females secured 60.4 percent of the passes and in St Vincent 61.1 percent.

These percentages and the ratio of gender achievement that they present are historically very interesting in that they indicate a reversal of educational tends in the last century. For example, Department of Education figures for Jamaica show that in 1988, 41.4 percent of high school enrolment was male compared with 58.5 percent female entry. This contrasts with corresponding figures for 1899 where 72.9 percent of high school enrolment was male compared to only 27.1 percent female.

These early figures are historically situated and reflect restricted educational opportunities for females compared to males and social attitudes which encompassed the notion that education was inappropriate for women. Where education was felt to be appropriate for females, it was highly selective and channelled them into areas which were thought necessary for their domestic and child-rearing propensities.

Indeed, today the legacy of those beliefs that structured educational opportunities for males and females in the last century is still apparent. Whilst examination results indicate that females are now performing overall at a higher level than previously, the statistics need to be treated with caution for a number of reasons. First, while females are undoubtedly doing better, they are still clustered primarily in subject areas that have traditionally been seen as female. So, for example, they do better than males in English but males are still more visible, and do better than females, in physics (Whitely 1994).

Second, although females seem to utilize education as an agent of social mobility more successfully than males, there remain glaring inequalities in the occupational structure once they leave school. Social mobility studies have indicated (Gordon 1986, 1989) how females are more socially mobile than males in the Caribbean, in that their socioeconomic status of destination is more likely to be different from their socioeconomic status of origin. However, whilst education constitutes an important agent of social mobility in the Caribbean, patterns of employment remain a function of gender inequality (Barrow 1988). Taking the class composition of the labour force, women, who are more likely to be in the middle strata, are heavily concentrated in the lower status and lower paid occupations and in the mass professions. Furthermore, within the professions it is men who monopolize higher and better paid positions. For example, although women dominate the teaching profession they are significantly underrepresented in headships. This disparity becomes more noticeable further up the academic scale, and particularly within the university structure (Drayton 1991).

American and British research suggests that social groups of pupils who are aware that they face a job ceiling, or that they will be denied equal access to professional jobs, shape and channel their educational output accordingly (Mickelson 1992; Ogbu 1978; Willis 1977). However, whilst previous research suggests that both race and class can affect motivation, the same is not true of gender. On the contrary, poor occupational return on educational investment does not appear to depress either school performance or willingness to earn advanced degrees (Mickelson 1992). This raises two questions: Why when Caribbean males appear to have many advantages in the occupational structure do they perform badly in school and, conversely, why when they face many disadvantages in the occupational structure do Caribbean females continue to strive to do well in education?

The study started from the premise that in order to understand why males were underachieving in some subjects, it was necessary to explore the gender educational related experiences and performances of both males and females. This is because any account that attempted to isolate the experience of either gender ran the risk of exploring only those aspects of educational experience that either encouraged or prohibited educational success.

The Study Methods

Choice of Methods

In the selection of research methods for this project several things were taken into account. The overriding concern was that the methods chosen should be those most suited to the task at hand. As the research focused upon what happened in classrooms then it seemed only natural to make schools and classrooms the centre of research activity. The study was also designed to ensure that the data collected would accurately reflect the interaction between teachers and pupils in a natural setting which had not been manipulated for experimental purposes and which as far as possible was undisturbed by the research.

In taking this approach the research was primarily influenced by the principles of naturalism and thus characterized by methods designed to find out why people do what they do, rather than just what they do. This was achieved by seeking to understand interaction in situ, as it occurred in its natural setting, and the meanings which it had for participants.

However, there were other things to be taken into account which put constraints upon what was feasible and possible. A major constraint was the level of resources available. The two most important resources that affected how this research was carried out were time and money, and these were inextricably linked. The length of the study was finite and it was the intention to complete it in less than two years. However, data collection was restricted to term time, and because of limited research assistance, data collection at each site was carried out sequentially. Because of this the study was actually completed in twenty-four months.

Time and money are not discrete entities. Had resources enabled the recruitment of a research team of assistants then the length of the project could have been shortened. As it was, only two researchers worked full-time during part of the data collection period and for the rest of the time only one researcher was working on the project full-time.

Time and money were not the only constraints; the methods themselves were important in setting the research agenda. As we shall see, ethnographic techniques that were used during the course of the research actually dictated how, where, when and in what sequence the data were collected.

The Research Sites

Because the study aimed to collect comparative data, the research design included more than one Caribbean territory. Given the time frame (of two years) and resources (for research assistance, travel and subsistence), the decision was made to include three research sites in the study. The next question was which ones to include.

If not a newcomer to educational research, as the principal researcher I was a newcomer to the Caribbean. Because of this, in the selection of research sites I relied heavily upon local available sources. First, data was needed on male underachievement in Caribbean territories other than Jamaica. This was achieved through an analysis of CXC records for examination results. Then I talked to Caribbean colleagues at the UWI, members of the Ministry of Education and the director of the CXC.

From the outset the intention was to select sites that shared some characteristics in common with each other yet at the same time differed in certain other respects. The main reason for this was methodological and related to the problem of generalizability. One issue raised by critics of qualitative research is representativeness. If we do research in one school or one classroom, what can this tell us, if anything, about any other school or even any other classroom in the same school? To what extent are we able to generalize from our data and to what extent can we extrapolate from any one setting to any other?

Issues of sampling and generalizability have been widely discussed by both qualitative and quantitative methodologists. Qualitative research demands very flexible sampling guidelines in order to observe the appropriate types of behaviours. Furthermore, qualitative researchers are concerned that their observations are not only typical of those they have studied but also could be generalized to other groups and individuals as well (Denzin 1978:77).

Any assessment of whether what is observed can be generalized to other settings must weigh issues relating to similarity and dissimilarity (Spindler 1982). In other words, in what way is the selected research site similar to, and in what way is it dissimilar from, other sites. Selection of respondents by virtue of characteristics such as age or sex or experience is often referred to as either judgement or purposeful sampling. This sampling method is familiar to qualitative researchers but it is important that the criteria used in the selection of respondents are made explicit

(Honigmann 1982; Hammersley 1984). It is also important that generalizability is applied not only to characteristics of members but also to aspects of physical settings in which interaction occurs and constraints which boundary behaviour therein (Hammersley and Atkinson 1983).

In defence of qualitative methods it can be argued that issues of generalizability are addressed, albeit somewhat differently from those using a positivist approach. There is no intention of qualitative research to emulate quantitative approaches through the random selection of either research sites or respondents. In qualitative research, sites are selected purposively and often on the basis of shared characteristics. However, they are also selected for their differences and techniques designed specifically to address the issue of generalizability are employed.

One such technique which was used to guide the selection of sites for this research is 'theoretical sampling' (Spradley 1980). Theoretical sampling allows the researcher to test out specific working hypotheses developed through data collection at one site, and at other sites which are selected because of both their differences to and similarities with our first research site.

Jamaica, Barbados, and St Vincent and the Grenadines comprised the three territories selected to take part in the research. Each selected with theoretical sampling in mind, they were similar to each other in some respects and differed in others. Jamaica and Barbados were selected to provide comparison of English-speaking territories that were campus sites of the UWI. They did, however, have contrasting levels of educational attainment with Barbados characteristically showing higher levels of attainment than Jamaica. Barbados also differed from Jamaica in that in the early 1980s all government single sex schools were amalgamated to make coeducational schools. Unlike Jamaica, Barbados has no government single sex schools.

St Vincent was selected because it is a small, English-speaking West Indian territory, which had single sex and coeducational schools, but was not a campus site of the UWI. It was also selected because the Ministry of Education in St Vincent had a highly centralized administrative function and schools were far less autonomous (in, for example, the selection and recruitment of teachers) than in either Barbados or Jamaica.

For the purposes of theoretical sampling, Jamaica was chosen as our main research site. This was where the initial research question arose and where the problem of male underachievement was most apparent. The Institute of Social and Economic Research (ISER), where the research funding was held and where the author was based, was located on the Mona campus of the UWI and this was yet another reason to select Jamaica as the main research site. The study was designed so that data collection was accomplished sequentially at each site starting in Jamaica. Upon completion of the Jamaican fieldwork, the research focus became Barbados and then St Vincent.

Using the technique of theoretical sampling, working hypotheses developed through the Jamaican data were explored at the other two sites. For example, the levels of gender-related achievement inequality were known to differ between the three territories and the research was interested in exploring the data to better understand those differences. The study was also interested in any implications that the totally coeducational environment of Barbados might have for gender-related achievement. Recruitment policies, specifically employed in St Vincent, which affected the gender ratio of teachers in the classroom became a further point of comparison between the different data sets.

Having selected the territories to be included, the next stage was deciding how many and what type of schools should be invited to participate. Again, the constraint of resources came into play. Given the time frame and the available level of research assistance, fifteen schools were selected to take part. In Jamaica, the largest territory, eight schools were identified. In Barbados, the second largest site, four schools were identified and a further three schools were identified in St Vincent. In addition to these fifteen schools which made up the main sample, a further two schools in the Grenadines were also included in the research.

All seventeen schools participating in the research were high schools. Those selected represented both rural and urban schools, and single sex and coeducational schools. Of the eight Jamaican schools that took part in the research, two were all-male schools, two were all-female schools and four were coeducational. In Barbados all government schools were coeducational; three of the four visited had previously been all-male schools and one had previously (prior to amalgamation) been an all-female school. In St Vincent one all-male school, one all-female school and one coeducational school participated in the research. Both schools in the Grenadines were coeducational.

Obtaining Access to Schools

A critical stage in any research programme is negotiating access. Individuals who are crucial in this negotiation are called 'gatekeepers' (Goffman 1968; Atkinson 1979; Parry 1990, 1992; Hammersley and Atkinson 1983) because they make the decision whether or not to allow researchers access to an organization or institution.

For this particular study it was necessary to obtain the permission of the Ministry of Education in each of the three territories before schools could be contacted. Access was a protracted process and because people seemed helpful but did not always follow through with their promises, delays were incurred which were characteristic of the early stages of most research (Burgess 1984).

Also, it routinely involves more than initial permission to enter. It is a continual and reflexive process. Even where permission is initially granted it may not be in accordance with the wishes of all members (Parry 1990). However, of the fifteen schools approached, only one head teacher denied research access and this was because of problems the school was facing at that time which had nothing to do with the research.

Upon gaining entry to schools, permission was also needed from teachers for observation and interviewing. Despite the fact that observation might appear threatening to teachers, and indeed many respondents expressed anxiety at having an observer in the classroom, only five teachers of all those we approached declined to participate in the research.

Ethical Considerations

One way of alleviating anxiety of respondents is through guarantees of anonymity. When approaching schools we assured heads that we would not release the names of participating institutions to the Ministry of Education, the funding body nor identify them in research reports or other publications. We gave the same assurances to all individuals who we observed and interviewed.

We also adhered closely to ethical codes in another important respect. At all stages of negotiation for access we were open about our research interests and provided ministries of education, heads of participating institutions, teachers and students with accounts of our research interests. In thus doing we conformed to the principle of 'informed consent' outlined by the British Sociological Society (1973) in their statement of practices and ethical codes. However, at the same time, we recognized that, while distancing ourselves from covert or 'secret' research, it is impossible to tell everyone everything all the time (Roth 1962). In other words, all research is covert to the extent that respondents are never in full knowledge of issues which interest the researcher at any one time in the research. Rather, they are made aware of the general areas of interest.

Recording Data

The initial intention had been to transcribe all the qualitative interviews. However, as it transpired, this was impractical on two counts. First, teachers were very wary about being tape recorded and when they did agree were much more hesitant to respond than when the tape recorder was turned off. Second, because teachers had little time in the school day and because schools had limited space, many of the interviews were conducted in busy, noisy places like staff rooms or form rooms during break times. For these two reasons the tape recorder was abandoned and conversations with respondents were, as far as possible, taken down verbatim during the interview.

Data Collection

The three main methods of data collection were classroom observation, qualitative or ethnographic style interviews with teachers, and self-completed pupil questionnaire schedules.

The research strategy adopted was as follows. First, a researcher carried out classroom observation. Following observation, teachers who had been observed were interviewed by the researcher at a time and place of the teacher's choice. At each participating school, one fourth form (approximately fifty students) was asked to complete questionnaire schedules.

Because the research was very labour intensive, observation in classrooms was limited to three subject areas and interviewing was restricted to teachers of those subjects. The subjects selected were English language, biology and physics. English was selected because it was a compulsory subject and also because it was the subject in which females traditionally excelled. The two science subjects, physics and biology, were selected as representing a science traditionally popular with males and females, respectively. At some schools, teachers of other subjects expressed a wish to participate in the research and we were pleased to accommodate them in this respect. At each site visited we interviewed fourth form teachers in the selected subjects, heads and guidance counsellors.

The lessons observed were fourth form lessons; teachers interviewed were fourth form teachers; and questionnaire respondents were fourth form pupils. The research focused upon this grade because entry into the fourth form directly followed students' selection of future examination subjects. Subject choices were important because they reflected preferences, abilities, influences of significant others and career planning.

In total, 110 interviews were carried out. These comprised seventeen heads, thirteen guidance counsellors and eighty-two teachers. Of the eighty-two teachers, thirty-four taught English, twenty-one taught biology and twenty taught physics. The remainder taught other arts, integrated science and vocational subjects.

Men constituted 29.5 percent of all teachers interviewed; the lowest percentage of male teachers interviewed was in Jamaica (24 percent). Of the seventeen head teachers, ten were male whereas twelve of the thirteen guidance counsellors were female. In the Caribbean female teachers outnumber male teachers and our sample broadly reflects the gender ratio of teachers.

The majority of teachers interviewed were observed teaching fourth form pupils prior to being interviewed.

Observation

Although the researchers aimed to observe all teachers who consented to take part in the research before conducting the interview this was not always feasible. The interviewees who had been observed were questioned about specific incidents which had taken place during the observation period, and they themselves also raised and talked about incidents which had been witnessed by the observer during their lessons. These interviews yielded the richest data, enabling triangulation of data (Denzin 1978) from the different data sources. Data from completed interviews and during observation was also useful for guiding questions and areas of interest in subsequent interviews and alerting the researcher to incidents occurring during observation. This reflexive approach guided the research inquiries into areas of mutual interest for both respondents and the researcher and helped overcome some of the initial difficulties routinely encountered by observers in any setting (Hammersley 1984; Olesen and Whittaker 1968).

Field notes recorded during observation were analysed and used to inform areas which were explored with teachers during interviews. In the interviews a questionnaire schedule was not used, nor were questions asked or issues raised in any particular order. Instead, conversations were initiated and stimulated around issues that emerged as important. In order to ensure these issues were covered, the researcher used an 'aide memoir' in the interviews (Burgess 1984). Areas probed in the interviews included background information on teachers (length and type of experience), aspects of classroom behaviour, motivation and performance, and pupil/teacher relationships.

The majority of the respondents were very forthcoming during the interviews and many said they appreciated the opportunity to talk about their experiences. Other researchers (Hammersley and Atkinson 1983) note similar responses for interviewees who value the interview as an opportunity of telling someone how they see the world.

The Questionnaires

Questionnaires were completed by pupils from one fourth form at each of the fifteen schools which made up the main sample. Questionnaires are not usually popular with qualitative researchers and particularly ethnographers (Woods 1986) because they limit the responses available to respondents. However, they have their uses. Given resource constraints, the questionnaires enabled the collection of some data from fourth form students at the research sites and thus provided useful comparative data.

For the most part, the selection of questionnaire respondents was left to head teachers because schools organized their fourth forms along different lines. Some fourth forms were ability streamed, some streamed according to subject choices (that is, arts, science and business) and some were not streamed. Head teachers were asked to select forms that they felt would be most representative of fourth formers as a whole.

In total, 668 questionnaire schedules were completed. The schedules provided some demographic data about students and focused upon their educational choices, future occupational plans and what they saw as major influencing factors in their lives. The schedules, which for the most part required pre-coded quantifiable responses, also contained some open-ended questions, the responses to which were analysed and coding categories devised accordingly.

Data Analysis

Data analysis was not postponed until the fieldwork was completed but started early into data collected and was ongoing throughout the fieldwork period. The research design subscribed to the practice of "grounded theory" (Glaser and Strauss 1967), treating data collection as a reflexive process through which working hypotheses were tested and reworked continuously. Guided by grounded theory the researcher entered the field with working hypotheses, collected data and withdrew to reflect upon how the data informed the initial hypothesis. After reworking the hypothesis in light of the data the researcher re-entered the field. This was a continuous process throughout fieldwork – theories are grounded in the actual data collected.

Upon the completion of data collection in Jamaica, a three-month period of data analysis allowed adequate preparation for data collection at the subsequent two sites, Barbados and St Vincent. These were the sites selected to explore the working hypotheses which had emerged out of the data collection in Jamaica.

The qualitative data, field notes from observation and interview data, were transcribed into ETHNOGRAPH, a computer software package well established among qualitative researchers as a useful analytic tool for facilitating the storage and retrieval of large qualitative data sets in a comprehensive and systematic fashion.

Questionnaire data was coded and analysed using SPSS (Statistical Package for the Social Sciences) and the responses were used to reflect upon the qualitative observation and interview material we collected inside and outside of classrooms. The triangulation of data in this way aimed at providing a more rounded account of attitudes, behaviours and beliefs of classroom participants.

Background to the Research

The study was theoretically influenced by interactionist social theory because it set out to understand classroom interaction not as a given but as the outcome of interaction, interpretation and negotiation. At the same time, the researchers recognized how classroom interaction did not occur in a vacuum but was informed, among other things, by constraints of history, ethnicity, biology, socioeconomics and environment.

In locating classroom interaction in the context of schools, cultural expectations and wider societal structures which operated as mediators of power and social control (Bernstein 1977), the study did not hold teachers solely responsible for the production and reproduction of gender divisions. Conversely, it concurred with Stanworth's (1983) contention that classroom interaction should be explored as an indicator or reflection of the much wider societal experiences and expectations in which it is embedded.

Given the research focus upon males, the research explored the relationship between male gender identity and educational performances. It was fully compatible with an interactionist tradition that gender identities were not interpreted as the manifestation of inner essences but seen as socially constructed as well as historically shifting (Kimmel 1996).

Furthermore, the study was based upon the understanding that there are multiple competing masculinities, only one of which achieves ascendancy at any particular historical junction. Connell (1995) (borrowing Antonio Gramsci's use of hegemony from his analysis of class relations) describes the ascendant masculinity as hegemonic masculinity. For both Gramsci and Connell, hegemony refers to a cultural dynamic by which a group claims and sustains a leading position in social relationships.

Hegemony, however natural in appearance, is arrived at via the social processes of competition, domination, subordination and resistance. From within this struggle hegemonic masculinity emerges as the configuration of gender practice which legitimates patriarchy and guarantees a dominant position for men alongside the subordination of women.

Caribbean historian Hilary Beckles (1996) describes the historical dimension of black Caribbean masculinities by locating them within the hegemonic white patriarchal institution of chattel slavery. Beckles suggests that hegemonic masculinity in the West Indies is associated with the possession of power, profits, glory and pleasure, all of which are articulated as core elements of a white masculine ideology in which, historically, black masculinity was negated and relegated to 'otherness'.

In the quest for control over masculinity, white slave owners employed two key strategies: the denial of black men to the right of patriarchal status, and the sexual appropriation of black females. Both strategies, exercised through violent regimes, effectively deprived black males of domestic authority as either husbands or fathers.

In relegating black males to a state of 'otherness', Beckles notes that in slave owner literature, infantilization linked closely with feminization in the conceptualization of both black slaves and white and black women. The black man, by virtue of being denied masculine roles or access to institutionalized support systems on which to construct counter-concepts, was conceived to have degenerated into preconsciousness, a condition that Beckles associates with nothingness, innocence and femininity.

The historical impact of hegemonic masculinity has implications for the importance that Caribbean males attach to the exercise of power and control over women (Johnson 1996). Very recent ethnographic research carried out in Jamaican, Dominican and Guyanese communities suggests that 'manhood' is attested by sexual prowess, usually measured in terms of numbers of serial or concurrent female sexual partners. Secondary proof of 'manhood' resides in numbers of offspring whether inside or outside of a steady relationship. Furthermore, the women's liberation movement (as well as harsh economic realities and foreign media) are seen as contributors to the erosion of man's authority in the home and to power struggles between men and women. These struggles, apparent in group discussions in all the communities researched, seemed related most often to the growing economic independence of women (Brown 1995).

The shift in occupational roles and the capacity of women to be providers and breadwinners have challenged notions of Caribbean masculinity (Mohammed 1996), while allowing women to extend concepts of femininity. That is, perhaps at the root of male fear is that they are losing ground and privilege, that their manhood is threatened when they cannot fulfil what they see as the "God given and natural role of men."

This fear is the source of Caribbean black male marginalization described by Miller (1986, 1989, 1991). Miller's work on the marginalization of the black male has resonances with the emasculation thesis in which men are again victims of the dominant colonial order. The problem with this is that Miller works within a paradigm of male dominance, assuming that this ideology is a natural one which must obtain in society. He places the burden once again on the backs of women for emasculating men (Mohammed 1996). Supporters of the marginalizaton thesis understand male educational failure and female educational success as two sides of the same equation and interpret the former as a function of the latter. Miller's ideas have attracted considerable interest and sympathy in the Caribbean and I have argued elsewhere (Parry 1995, 1997) how they underlay discriminatory educational policies.

While Miller accurately observes that Jamaican women have taken advantage of educational opportunities and achieved greater mobility than men (Mohammed 1996), he does not question the notion of manhood itself and the way in which this may be at variance with the requirements of the education system. Lewis (1996) points out how male marginalization, which is mediated by factors of race, class, age and sexual orientation, is the product of changing socioeconomic and political considerations and not a wilful attempt (by women) to penalize men.

The research presented here explores some of the ways in which the Caribbean classroom offers male students an arena in which to develop and demonstrate masculinity through their educational responses. British research has suggested (Mac An Ghaill 1994; Haywood and Mac An Ghaill 1996; Weekes et al. 1996) a mismatch in the orientation of education and the way in which masculinities are perceived, and this may have serious implications for male educational achievement in the developing as well as the developed world.

For the purposes of this publication the data have been analysed and broken down into short sections. Each section explores aspects of gender-related responses and the relationship between teachers and pupils.

The following sections examine responses to verbal discipline, the perceived importance of male role models, perceived advantages of single sex education for males, gender responses and nature/nurture explanations, the development of sex/gender role identity and the relationship between male gender identity and educational outcomes. Although separated out for the purposes of analysis and presentation, the contents of the following sections are not discrete but overlap and inform all of the other sections to provide an interrelated account of gender performance.

The data presented were collected in schools. The boundary between home and school, however, should be understood as permeable and because of this classroom attitudes, behaviour and aptitudes should be interpreted as reflecting cultural attitudes, behaviour and expectations in which school-based performances are embedded.

Gender Expectations

Many heads, teachers and guidance counsellors who took part in the study felt that upon leaving school, males and females did not have equal opportunities in the occupational structure. Generally they felt that the occupational structure discriminated in favour of male school leavers. An English teacher from an urban girls' school in Jamaica describes below how awareness of this privilege discouraged male interest in schooling:

"More parents press their girls to do well in school and to become independent. It's a male oriented society. Even if a man is less educated than a woman, he will get a better job with more money. It's not surprising that boys aren't motivated at school."

Despite awareness that males may fare better than females upon leaving school, girls' educational efforts and achievements appeared to remain undaunted. An English teacher at an urban coeducational school in Jamaica pointed out how, despite all odds, females perform better than boys educationally:

"Girls do better (in school) and do better despite balancing the numbers of high school places. However, I recognize that men are at the top in this society, they have the best jobs and if there's competition between a man and a woman the man will get it."

Interestingly, the converse was said about males. The guidance counsellor at a rural coeducational school suggested that actual awareness that the odds were stacked in their favour predisposed male pupils to underachieve in school:

"Most of the boys I would describe as mediocre. They feel that they will get a job when they leave school despite their poor performance."

Males have high expectations upon leaving school. They expect to get better jobs with more money than their female peers, in spite of perhaps having lower educational qualifications. The librarian at a Jamaican rural school for females explained how occupations which are largely filled by women hold little attraction for males, who saw them as inferior and low status:

"I don't know what the boys are looking forward to. They look out there and see a lot of women doing the jobs which they might have wanted to do; that men used to do. They see this in teaching and they don't want to be a teacher because they see it as a lesser position. They don't want to earn the same money as a woman."

Certainly money appeared to be a critical factor in career choice, even more so for the males than the females. Of the pupils, 67.3 percent males compared to 59.7 percent females who completed questionnaires described salary as very important in their choice of future occupation. In the interviews with heads, teachers and counsellors, salary was frequently raised around the issue of 'men' and 'women's' work. The head of an urban boys' school suggested that rather than accept a low salary males might be tempted into unorthodox and illegal means of obtaining an income. This attitude was expressed as "anything rather than have to do a woman's job":

"I have a feeling that it might have something to do with the status of equity and salary. If both men and women do a degree they get the same salary. Many men see this as an affront. So they move into trading to bypass it. You know what I mean by trading because I'm not going to spell it out! Many of these boys come from the ghetto and they see jewellery and trinkets and they are impressed. Education is not going to get them what they want so they bypass it."

That the occupational structure was felt by educationalists to favour men over women undoubtedly affected their attitudes to the educational motivation of males at school. It was perhaps unsurprising that male pupils were described by respondents as having a "something for nothing attitude". The difference between this attitude and that of female pupils was described by a male biology teacher at a rural coeducational school:

"It's an attitude with the boys. They don't want to or they don't expect to have to work for their rewards. They expect to have life offered to them on a plate. Girls don't have this attitude. They are motivated to get out there and achieve something."

Responses from the pupil questionnaire schedules indicated that 76.9 percent of female pupils compared to 63.5 percent of male pupils felt that personal betterment was very important in their choice of future career. Conversely, whereas 17.8 percent of male pupils indicated that personal fame was very important in their future career choice this compared to only 7.4 percent of the female pupils.

Divisions and inequalities in domestic responsibilities was thought by respondents to further reinforce the unequal opportunity structures for women and men. A guidance counsellor at a rural coeducational school suggested:

"It's different for a boy. When a boy leaves school and goes out, he gets a job. He can stay 'x' amount of hours at work progressing in his career whereas the girl is looking after his home and the children, she doesn't have the hours to spend working for her career. So the man goes higher and higher than the woman. Once a girl gets pregnant that's really the end of that for her."

Our respondents also felt that males rejected the education system because many had aspirations of "going foreign", upon leaving school. Respondents felt that having family members living in Canada, America and Britain may prompt male pupils to dismiss their current educational experiences as invalid. Interestingly, this argument for educational underachievement was only offered by respondents for males.

Data from the pupil questionnaires indicated the difference in responses of females and male pupils on this subject were not that great. Of those pupils who said they intended to continue education upon leaving high school, overall 35.3 percent said they wished to pursue their studies outside of the Caribbean. Of the female respondents, 35.9 percent wished to study abroad compared to 44.5 percent of male students. When asked where they saw themselves spending most of their adult lives, 41.1 percent of the females and 47.8 percent of males said Britain, Canada or America.

Furthermore, the contention that males would have an easier time in the occupational structure, which may once have been a reality, was seen as currently questionable. Unemployment was high and some respondents, like the teacher from St Vincent cited below, recognized the difficulties which males face upon leaving school:

"Well it's not as if they've got a lot to look forward to. Maybe fishing and maybe in the hotels but other than that there is very little here for them."

The changing demands of global economic and occupational structures have implications for all educational systems, and the Caribbean is by no means exempt. However, the discrepancies between students' aspirations and perceptions of what is actually achievable through education affects both males and females. Unlike males, and despite inequalities they may face in the occupational structure upon leaving school, it seems that females continue to use the education system as a vehicle for social mobility.

The following sections explore aspects of school practices and classroom interaction and the implications of gender-differentiated educational responses for academic performances.

The Use of Verbal Discipline

During the interviews, teachers described differences between the classroom behaviour of male and female pupils, and these descriptions supported our own observations in the classroom. In comparison to females, who for the most part appeared orderly and diligent, males were often boisterous, disruptive and easily distracted in class. The distinction was highlighted by both male and female teachers and is captured below by a Jamaican teacher at an urban coeducational school:

"In the fourth form although girls become more noisy their noise is different to the boys' noise. They will say out aloud 'slow down you're going too fast, could you say that again, I don't understand that miss'. That is their kind of noisiness. The noise that boys make, on the other hand, prompts me to say 'shut up and pay attention'."

Male and female teachers in Jamaica, Barbados and St Vincent used adjectives like 'attentive', 'applied', 'serious' and 'encouraging' to describe female pupils' attitudes to classroom work and adjectives like 'lazy', 'disruptive' and 'noisy' to describe the male pupils' attitudes to work.

Despite this, and despite the fact that females were educationally outperforming males, overwhelmingly, female teachers in all three territories claimed to prefer teaching males to females. Furthermore, female teachers in the Caribbean felt males were easier to teach than females. A female teacher in a Jamaican rural coeducational classroom described how she found misbehaviour from female students more difficult to handle than from males:

"Boys just put their heads down and go to sleep whereas the girls are masters of deception. The main thing is the maliciousness, they hold it up against you. It's an attitude. An attitudinal (sic) way they talk to you."

The behaviour of female pupils, which teachers felt rendered them more difficult to teach, materialized in *personal attitude* which they described as 'rude', 'less straightforward', 'petty', 'malicious' and 'personal'. These adjectives were not used to describe male students, who were depicted as more straightforward, easier to discipline and less resentful than their female peers, who at one extreme provoked a Jamaican teacher to say:

"Boys are much easier to discipline than girls. Unlike the girls, the boys don't have any bitterness or feeling they are being victimized. Girls have a bitchy resentfulness which lingers with them. They are more difficult to handle, although the boys do more violent things than the girls."

It is interesting that the above account was provided by a female teacher at an urban boys' school who had no experience of teaching female pupils.

The contrasting gender responses described by female teachers were inevitably linked to the issue of verbal discipline in the classroom and were summed up by a female teacher in a coeducational school in St Vincent:

"If you tell a boy off he will have forgotten about it the next day. If you tell a girl off she may remind you about it four years on when she's left school."

Male teachers did not appear to experience these problems with female students and many said they preferred to teach female students who were "more motivated and less disruptive", than their male peers. Many male teachers were also critical of the way in which female teachers treated female students. Some felt, for example, that their female colleagues were "too hard on the girls", set "very high standards for the girls", and that they were "very strict, particularly with female students". Male teachers appeared to avoid some of the problems that female colleagues experienced with female pupils, and the way they did this was to treat them differently than male students. In this respect, some male teachers said that they attempted to "avoid upsetting the girls" by "not talking to them or treating them in the same way", while others simply said they tended to "smile at them a lot more".

Conversely, our female respondents were largely adamant that they treated male and female students equally despite their perception that "if you treat girls and boys in an identical way then they will still react differently" (Barbadian female teacher).

Because verbal discipline was the issue around which female teachers constructed gender distinctive responses, it is important to understand the dynamics of classroom discipline as they are enacted in the Caribbean high school classroom. In the following extract from field notes, a typical instance of the teacher/pupil interaction which was observed during the study is played out in a Barbados classroom:

The teacher stands at the front of the class and calls on a particular male student, who is not paying attention to the teacher, to answer a question. The student clearly does not know the answer and attempts to attract the attention of the boy next to him for assistance. The teacher, upon detecting this, snaps 'This is a case of the blind trying to lead the blind. And in this case your friend is so blind I don't know if he'll ever see again.' Both boys remain silent and avert their gaze from the teacher.

We observed that sarcasm was used routinely as a disciplinary strategy by teachers in the schools we visited. We also noticed that female teachers resorted to sarcasm more readily than the male teachers we observed and the latter rarely used sarcasm as a strategy for disciplining female students.

Unlike their male peers, teachers perceived female students as being more responsive to classroom discipline. The male teacher from Barbados cited below describes differences in the way in which male and female pupils respond to discipline:

"Girls are more responsive. If you discipline a girl or reprimand her she will respond but a boy will ignore you. He'll just shrug and say 'What him know?' It's a very male thing to stand up to discipline."

The majority of teachers who participated in the research felt that the different gender responses to verbal discipline reflected fundamental differences between male and female pupils. Our data, however, suggest an alternative explanation. Rather than being the result of natural gender distinctions, gender classroom responses tend to reflect cultural expectations about the very different ways in which males and females are expected to respond. These cultural expectations are translated into pedagogical practices and become part of routine teacher/pupil interaction.

Teachers, and female teachers in particular, clearly expect male pupils to cope with verbal chastisement, and sarcasm in particular, differently than female students. The key to why males accept a style of verbal discipline that females reject is rooted in cultural expectations of how males and females are supposed to respond. In the Caribbean, cultural expectations of male behaviour are informed by an extremely hard, macho, masculine sex/gender identity, which is associated with maleness.

This masculine sex/gender identity informs classroom behaviour, motivation and educational performance. I have argued elsewhere (Parry 1995, 1997) that male sex/gender identity, as it is currently conceived, whilst being encouraged in the Caribbean classroom runs contrary to the academic ethos of schooling because it dismisses educational efforts and achievements as 'sissy', 'effeminate' and 'nerdish'.

In an environment in which males were prohibited from demonstrating what are seen to be 'female responses', it was not surprising that males tended to exhibit the 'water off a duck's back' attitude to verbal disciplining so often described by the respondents. Indeed, two of our more enlightened respondents felt that teachers misread male students' reaction to disciplining strategies. In the following account, a female teacher in Barbados describes how male students were expected to be insensitive:

"Teachers do treat girls and boys differently and there is a definite tendency to treat boys as if they have no feelings whatsoever. Boys do hurt, can be hurt by words and actions of a teacher."

The St Vincent teacher cited below demonstrated a level of insight into disciplining strategy which was rare among our respondents:

"I am aware that before I did my degree I used sarcasm as one form of discipline control. I never do that now; I think it is particularly damaging. Too many teachers assume that children can take it, especially the boys, but I think it hurts them just the same. I see it with my own sons. Boys appear tougher because they are taught not to show their feelings or express emotions. Boys don't cry, they learn this from an early age."

Many more teachers failed to recognize how male responses to verbal chastisement, and sarcasm in particular, may be less a function of the level of male tolerance and insensitivity and more a function of affirmation of masculine sex/gender identity. Previous research suggests that sarcasm and ridicule as a disciplinary strategy in the classroom can be extremely counterproductive and provoke all kinds of student retaliation (Ritchie and Ritchie 1981; Wilson 1982; Woods 1975). Indeed, it mitigates academic effectiveness in a number of ways (Woods 1975). It can provoke resentment among pupils and a desire for revenge as well as dislike for the teacher, the subject and maybe school in general. It may, in the long term, reinforce anti-teacher peer group attitudes and contribute to a climate of tension and hostility in the classroom (Woods 1975; Lewis and Lovegrove 1987). There are numerous studies supporting these views (Gaskell 1960; Furlong 1977; Galwey 1970; Raven 1976), including research carried out in secondary schools in Barbados (Payne 1988). In a questionnaire survey of students Payne found that verbal ridicule was rejected as vehemently as corporal punishment and led to a lack of trust and disrespect for teachers involved.

Previous research therefore suggests that styles of verbal discipline have an important impact upon educational performance. If it is the case that male pupils disguise or internalize their responses to forms of verbal discipline currently used in Caribbean classrooms then this will have serious implications for levels of male educational achievement.

The research findings did suggest that the gender-differentiated responses to verbal discipline were most extreme in Jamaican classrooms. Although teachers from all three territories described gender-related differences, it was the Jamaican respondents who problematized the responses to a greater extent. The field notes certainly suggested that the use of sarcasm and ridicule as disciplinary strategies was more widespread in the Jamaican schools that participated in the research.

Accordingly, we hypothesized that the usage of sarcasm and ridicule was related to the level of teacher training which our respondents had received. We found that the Jamaican teachers were the least trained of the respondents from all three territories. Of the Jamaican teachers, 39.6 percent had no teaching qualification, although the majority of these non-trained teachers (91 percent) were graduates. Non-graduate, teacher trained were 22.4 percent and 36.9 percent were graduates with a teaching qualification. Two teachers were high school graduates. In comparison, the Barbadian teachers were the most highly trained. All the trained teachers (82.1 percent of the sample) were graduates and 17.9 percent were non-teacher trained graduates. The St Vincent teachers fell somewhere in between the two: 55.5 percent were teacher trained and 75 percent of these teachers were also graduates. Thirty-seven percent were non-teacher trained graduates and the remaining two teachers were high school graduates. Given that gender-differentiated responses to verbal discipline were most extreme in Jamaica, it seems likely that training had implications for teacher pupil interaction in this respect.

The Issue of Male Role Models

Many of the heads, teachers and guidance counsellors who were interviewed described how masculine or macho attitudes and behaviour were not compatible with either educational motivation or good grades. At the same time, however, they expressed deep concern, which echoes international anxiety (Elliot 1995), that the development of male sex/gender identity is threatened by a lack of suitable male role models.

In the Caribbean context, part of this concern stems from the large number of single parent female-headed family units. Responses from our questionnaires indicated that, overall, 58.9 percent of pupils who took part in the survey lived in households having both mother and father present; 30.8 percent lived in households that were single parent, female headed, compared to only 4.4 percent that were single parent, male headed. A breakdown across the three territories indicated that the group having the highest single parent, female-headed households were the Barbadian respondents (33.3 percent), followed closely by St Vincentian respondents (32.7 percent) and then by the Jamaican respondents (29.6 percent).

Many of the heads, counsellors and teachers interviewed were concerned about the adverse effects of absentee fathers on attitudes and behaviour of adolescent males and some clearly held mothers responsible:

"You know, in Jamaica it is the women who are wrecking the men. In this society most households don't have men . . ."

The high occurrence of households lacking a male parent or guardian is compounded by the fact that there are many more female teachers than male teachers in the Caribbean. In our sample, men constituted 29.5

percent of all teachers interviewed; the lowest percentage of male teachers interviewed was in Jamaica (24 percent). Of the seventeen head teachers, ten were male whereas twelve of the thirteen guidance counsellors were female. Although the respondents were not randomly selected, in the Caribbean female teachers outnumbered male teachers and our sample broadly reflected the gender ratio of teachers.

Both male and female respondents talked about an "overpresence of female teachers" in schools. The invisibility of male teachers, it was argued, failed to redress the absence of a father figure in the home. This was held by the male head of an urban boys' school in Jamaica to be particularly salient for the boys from single parent female-headed households:

"I think it's good for the boys to have exposure to male teachers and I'm happy about their presence in the school. Many of the boys lack a male father figure at home."

Respondents felt that "schools have too many women teachers", and that "boys are sick of seeing women". This concern was stressed by head teachers, including the female head of an urban boys' school in Jamaica:

"Of the 66 teachers I have, 9 are men. I try to attract men but I don't discriminate in recruitment."

Single parent, female-headed households and a predominance of female teachers were felt to compound problems that boys experienced in developing appropriate male sex/gender identity.

There are several reasons for challenging this thinking. The first is that previous research has shown that it is often an erroneous supposition that female single parent family units do not have access to role models from which children can learn (Epstein 1993; Stack 1974). Furthermore, research also suggests there is no firm basis to assume boys who grow up in fatherless families are more likely as men to suffer from masculine identity as a result of lacking role models (Herzog and Sudia 1971).

More recent international research focuses on the way in which fathers, rather than contributing to traditional masculine identity, may usefully help to break it down via supportive caring roles (Mac An Ghaill 1994). Our data support this position, given that masculine gender identity, as it exists in its present construction, appears detrimental to the educational interests of Caribbean males.

Furthermore, any link made between fatherless families and poor educational performance of boys should consider home and school research in this area, just as men and women have radically different experiences of family life (Bernard 1982). So, there are two types of parent/school relationships; his and hers (Laureau 1992). In terms of schooling and relationships between the school, 'parents' invariably means mothers.

The contention, that it might be more appropriate to break down traditional masculine identity patterns in preference to reinforcing them, relates to a second point. This concerns teachers, and more specifically the underrepresentation of male teachers in school. Head teachers felt that male teachers tended to reinforce traditional masculine identities. In doing so, they reinforced attitudes and behaviour that contradicted the academic ethos of the school. For example, the small numbers of male teachers were clustered in the 'traditional male' subjects such as physics and maths and virtually invisible in the arts subjects such as English.

Furthermore, male teachers at the schools in the study tended towards perpetuating gender stereotypical attitudes to subjects. The female head of a rural girls' school in Jamaica, for example, felt that male teachers, particularly in the sciences, held very rigid views about what constituted men's role in the school:

"I have a young graduate science teacher who will not correct English errors of pupils because he says he is a science teacher and it's not his job. He's not the only one who won't pay attention to language skill because it's a woman's subject. They refuse to use English themselves when they set and mark work. We are having some problems with this right now. So many students, and particularly men, cannot cope with English when they get to university."

This raises an interesting point in regard to 'masculinity' and the teaching role. Connell (1985) writes about the apparent incompatibility between conventional positioning of femininity and the disciplinary role of teacher, in that authority is associated with masculinity. Leaving aside the issue that authority may not be seen as compatible with femininity, Connell's point is of relevance here because it highlights the fact that the teaching role is not unambiguously masculine. This is because it concerns emotional involvement and caring, which are usually defined as women's domain. The classroom, argues Connell, is not designed to cope with emotional ambiguity which may challenge traditional gender roles of men as strong and women as vulnerable and emotional. Equally so, the male teacher role may be resilient to the blurring of gender divisions; divisions that perpetuate particular educational interests and skills as women's work.

This point was reinforced by several of the heads we talked to, who expressed concern that men who were attracted into teaching were not necessarily the most appropriate role models for male pupils, and is captured thus by the male head of a rural coeducational school:

"Where boys are performing well there's usually a father at home. In theory, I think male teachers could be role models but, really, not all of them are qualified to be role models. Role models who are strong get the best results from the boys."

Ironically, while the absence of male teachers was lamented by heads, the research findings suggested the teaching role was not compatible with the construction of masculinity to which Jamaican males aspire. Respondents described how male teachers often became targets for suspicion among their female colleagues, quite simply because in their eyes they did not qualify as 'real men'. If this is so, it would be unlikely that male teachers could supply the appropriate role model which many respondents felt to be crucial to educational performance of male pupils.

Teaching in the Caribbean has not always been seen as a female occupation. Ministry of Education figures for Jamaica demonstrated a startling reversal of the gender ratio of teachers. In 1985, 17.7 percent of teachers were male, compared to 82.3 percent females teachers. In 1872 the figures indicate that 92.5 percent of teachers were male compared to only 7.5 percent female teachers.

Furthermore, our comparative research data demonstrates how teaching is not necessarily seen as 'women's work' even in the contemporary Caribbean. In many Caribbean territories (particularly Jamaica) teaching is unpopular among males because of the extremely poor level of remuneration and, not unrelated to this, the fact that it is primarily seen as 'women's work'. However, it was interesting that the 'feminization' of teaching was not uniformly offered across all three territories as a reason for male underachievement. In St Vincent, teaching appeared to be more popular among males for two reasons. Teachers in St Vincent were classified as civil servants and were relatively occupationally mobile within the wider civil service. That there were opportunities to move both vertically and horizontally in the occupational structure of the civil service attracted males into the occupation, particularly in the early stages of their careers. Also, many of the Vincentian respondents had or were in the process of obtaining higher qualifications through government-assisted funding. It was not unusual for teachers to have received their teaching qualifications and university degrees since entering teaching. Teaching, for Vincentians, was therefore a vehicle for occupational mobility and as such was utilized by both males and females. In this context, teaching avoided the level of ambiguity about gender roles which was reflected in data from Barbados and particularly Jamaica.

Coeducation Versus Single Sex Schools

Concern with the underachievement of males in education has raised questions about the advantages and disadvantages of single sex versus coeducational educational environments. Although there has been much research in this area, the results are highly contradictory and far from conclusive. Whereas some studies claim that males do better in single sex education (see, for example, Hamilton 1981), others (for example, see Dale 1962) claim the reverse.

Interestingly, the research findings as they relate to females appear to be less contradictory. Many studies indicate females do better in single sex education (Lee and Bryck 1988; MacMillan 1981; Riordan 1985) than in coeducation. However they also appear to adapt better than their male peers to coeducational settings (Walford 1983). It is beyond the scope of this publication, or the research on which it was based, to argue the case for either single sex or coeducation. However, certain aspects of the research do reflect upon issues that relate to the debate and it is those aspects that are discussed in this section.

Heads, teachers and guidance counsellors who took part in the research make clear distinctions between the responses of female and male pupils. The three areas in which gender-related distinctions were most clear were classroom behaviour, participation in class work and responses to verbal discipline.

Many respondents felt that male pupils would be educationally advantaged in all-male educational contexts. Such contexts, it was argued, would have a high percentage of male teachers who would provide suitable role models for sex/gender identity development. Furthermore, in an educational context made up exclusively of male peers, males would no longer be subject to the educationally intimidating (and distracting) presence of females.

However, as described in the previous section, our data also suggested that heads, teachers and counsellors were ambivalent about male staff members. Teaching was primarily still conceived of as 'women's work'. To reiterate, this is because it was seen as poorly paid and some aspects of the role, such as emotional support and caring, appeared to fall into the traditional female domain. Male teachers were often viewed with suspicion by their colleagues, because by definition it was debatable whether they qualified as 'real men'.

Furthermore, the argument that male pupils were adversely affected by the presence of female pupils in the classroom should be treated with caution. We found little difference in the behaviour of male pupils in the single sex and coeducational classrooms we visited. Certainly, we observed that males were no less concerned, in the single sex context, about being shown up in front of other males. Displays of hard male macho behaviour were equally apparent in the single sex and coeducational schools and likewise appeared to affect classroom performance accordingly.

Recent research suggests that the audience to which displays of maleness are directed are primarily made up of other males (Kimmel 1996) and are prompted by a fear of being unmasked as a fraud by male peers. If this is so then the exclusively male environment may serve to reinforce the male sex/gender identity which currently appears to run contrary to the academic aims of education.

A study on coeducation has been carried out in Barbados by Hazel Carrington (1993). Carrington collected data from one school (pre, during and post amalgamation of two separate single sex schools to a coeducational school) and looked for relationships between sex composition, CEE scores, socioeconomic status and sex of pupils.

Overall, Carrington found no significant differences between achievements in the single sex and coeducational setting for males (although she found females did significantly better after the amalgamation). However, it did highlight the very negative expectations held by teachers about the effects of coeducation on males. Furthermore, male pupils in the study who had experienced the amalgamation clearly felt that coeducation impacted negatively upon the way they were treated by teachers.

Carrington concluded that teachers may not be aware that they treat girls and boys differently, a point that substantiates our findings that teachers have very clear and distinct expectations about how males and females ought to behave.

Particularly in Barbados, many respondents who were interviewed highlighted the advantages of single sex education, especially for boys. Despite the fact that schools in Barbados were amalgamated to form coeducational institutions sixteen years ago, many teachers in Barbados still talked about "girls going to boys' schools", and "boys going to girls' schools".

It appeared that the transition from single sex to coeducational schooling in Barbados had been a long and difficult one. Some respondents still talked about the stigma attached to "boys going to girls' schools" (which appeared to have much greater stigma attached to it than "girls going to boys' schools"), a stigma that reflects the early days of the transition, described by a Barbados head:

"Also parents who elected to send boys here tended to choose us because their boys were frail or delicate in health (asthmatic) or sensitive. Boys' schools were, in comparison to this school, rough places to be."

The findings of the study highlighted a concern among educationalists that teachers' expectations about non-academic aspects of behaviour might be mitigating the educational responses of males in the coeducational context. In the previous section some discussion was provided about teacher expectation and verbal disciplining in the classroom. In the coeducational context, respondents in Barbados described how (female) teachers experienced problems with male students, particularly following amalgamation.

Some educationalists clearly felt that the high levels of control and strictness which indexed the relationship between (female) teachers and (female) pupils were inappropriate for male pupils. Furthermore, the disruption of the 'male' culture of education, which boys had previously experienced (in the single sex setting), were felt to have caused problems of adjustment for both pupils and teachers after amalgamation.

Some aspects of 'noisiness' along with the physical manifestation of exercise in the form of sweat were assessed. Female teachers were criticized by male teachers (and by some female teachers) for expecting the 'same high, standards' from male pupils as they were used to expecting from females. A male teacher in Barbados describes below the exacting standards of deportment and appearance demanded by (some) female teachers:

"The boys are different to the girls in that they are rougher. They sweat a lot. They can come into class soaking wet. Now, some teachers don't like that. You never see girls looking like that. Some teachers see it as rude."

Conversely, similar problems were raised in respect to male teachers upon confronting female pupils for the first time:

"You can't use the same methods for boys. Teachers of boys only can't do this in coed classrooms. They use a level of profanity which is unacceptable and they will hit a child. I know of cases where altercations between two male pupils has been resolved by the teacher taking the boys outside and telling them to settle their differences using fists. Of course, that teacher wouldn't have dreamt of doing that to girls or find it appropriate in the coed setting" (Barbadian male teacher).

What is surprising about both these sets of problems is not that they occurred but that they persisted in occurring so long after amalgamation. The research suggested, therefore, that in Barbados, schools and their participants (both teachers and pupils) were ill prepared for amalgamation. Problems like the ones outlined above should have been anticipated and resolved prior to and during the amalgamation period.

Another factor that should be taken into account when assessing the advantages and disadvantages of single sex education for males relates to the level of entry. When schools amalgamated in Barbados, some institutions lowered the entry requirement for males to ensure that male pupils were represented in significant proportions. A similar policy operated in Jamaica at the time of the research. That is, in order to ensure males were represented in high school, a policy of positive discrimination was being practised. This effectively meant that females had to score more points than males in the CEE to receive a high school place. Although many respondents defended this policy (on the grounds that at the time the test is sat, females have reached a higher level of maturity than boys), others, like this teacher from Barbados, pointed to disadvantages:

"Even after fourteen years this policy persists. So we got the boys who couldn't get into Harrison College and they weren't as bright as our girls. Obviously, they may as a result have trouble educationally competing with the girls."

Despite the argument that boys eventually catch up with the girls, some respondents pointed out that boys might well be aware that upon entry into high school their female peers perform at higher levels:

"I think the boys know that the girls are better than them when they get to high school and I think psychologically this is very bad for them."

Gender Socialization: Issues of Nature and Nurture

This section explores some aspects of gender socialization occurring both inside and outside of school. The relationship between the home and the school is a familiar topic to educational researchers who have used indicators such as family type as a prediction of level of resources available to children. For example, sex distribution, number and age of children, family type (nuclear or expanded), social kin networks, marital conflict and father involvement (De Marris and Greif 1992).

Heads, teachers and counsellors in this study described two patterns of gender socialization in the Caribbean: one for males and one for females. This supports the ethnographic findings of UNICEF-funded research carried out by Brown and Chevannes (1995) which focused upon male gender socialization in Jamaica, Dominica and Guyana.

The respondents in our study described how once outside the school gates male and female pupils were subject to quite different socialization patterns and these are captured by the "tie the heifer, loose the bull" analogy, used by Chevannes and Brown's Guyanese respondents. Whereas males were described as "free" and "without responsibility" outside of school, females were described as "restricted" and "home bound". There are several implications for the differences between male and female socialization in this respect.

The first stems from the "need to protect girls", described by many of our respondents. We were repeatedly told that "girls can't do what the boys do". Consequently, young females are largely restricted to 'the yard' (home) whereas males are free to roam on the 'street'. This is important because, as we shall see, teachers' understanding of gender differences in school were embedded in the social and cultural experience of pupils outside of school. For example, many respondents said that the home experiences of female pupils prepared them for responsibility in a way that home experiences of male pupils did not. This supports recent research (cited by Handra 1994) indicating the extent to which daughters in Jamaica are expected to look after younger siblings. The responsibility, acquired through domestic duties which females were expected to carry out at home, was one from which the boys largely escaped:

"It has to do with enculturalization, that's why girls work better. Girls all have duties at home. They have to cook the breakfast, make the beds and look after younger children. Boys don't do these duties. When you've got duties it helps you to focus. You do what you have to do. You learn to manage yourself" (Jamaican female teacher).

Another female teacher, cited below, describes the different expectations for Jamaican males and females:

"Girls learn to be more responsible. They do dishes and wash clothes. So women pass on this message. Boys are largely carefree and not responsible."

A similar view was expressed below by a teacher from St Vincent:

"Girls' leisure time is structured much more around the home. They have a lot more domestic responsibility in the home. Sometimes the boys don't feel as if they have to do anything."

Indeed, males are actively encouraged to socialize outside on the street:

"Boys are encouraged to go outside and time for playing is seen as very important for boys" (Barbadian teacher).

Respondents described the very different experiences of males and females outside of school and the development of quite different gender pastimes and interests. Educationally, the most important distinction noted by the respondents was that females read a lot more than males.

"Girls are encouraged to stay inside and read. It starts at an early age" (Vincentian teacher).

The view that the aptitude which females demonstrated toward reading was acquired in the home was shared by respondents from all three research sites and is reinforced below by a teacher from Barbados:

"Girls seem to have the academic edge in reading and that's because they do it a lot more."

That reading is largely seen as a female pastime has lead to its unpopularity among male students, who tend to see it as female, sissyish and nerdish. Hence the head of a rural coeducational school in Jamaica explained:

"Boys don't read because of our culture orientation. Reading is not macho or masculine enough for them. It's maybe too girlish."

This view was reinforced by many of our respondents, who interpreted gender differences in attitude towards reading as learnt behaviour:

"The girls read more. They don't see it as something they shouldn't do whereas the boys see it differently. They don't see it as something that boys should do. I think it is learnt behaviour. We don't want our boys to be sissy so we push them into macho behaviour."

Hence, males who show aptitude and interest in reading prefer to conceal this from their peers for fear of being seen as 'soft'. Teachers in all three territories talked about the way in which male pupils would conceal books and read in private away from the critical gaze of the peer group. This is captured below by a teacher from Barbados:

"If a boy likes reading he certainly won't show it. He'll do his reading somewhere else."

A teacher from St Vincent remarked:

"It's the way boys are bought up. I have watched parents seeing a boy reading and telling him to go outside and find something better to do."

Inside School

When at school, patterns of gender socialization may affect educational experiences in a number of ways. One important way explored above suggested that because females are 'less free', home based and have more domestic responsibilities than males, they are socialized into behaviour patterns that 'suit' schooling. They are, in other words, used to stricter discipline than males, must be more responsible in their actions, and are used to undertaking and completing designated tasks. In comparison, males are largely freed from the domestic responsibilities that fall to their sisters and they lack the regime of discipline which respondents felt advantaged females at school.

The other way in which gender socialization outside of school appeared to advantage females was that they were more likely than males to engage in what was repeatedly described to us as the 'female pastime' of reading. Not only English teachers but teachers in all three subjects explored by the study felt that reading and writing skills were fundamentally important to educational performance in other subjects.

Teachers complained that male pupils did not read routinely and that the "presentation skills of the boys is very sloppy". Science teachers particularly felt that whilst male pupils displayed an 'aptitude' for the subject, when writing results of experiments and in other presentation skills, they were lacking. This contrasted with teachers' descriptions of female pupils' work as "more thorough", "neater" and "more acceptable" than the males.

A separate but related point is the extent to which patois is used in preference to 'standard English' both in the home and in school. Educationalists in the study recognized that patois as the "language of the school yard" embodies the hard, macho image with which many young males identify. At the same time, however, standard English was the language of the school.

The problem here is complicated as not all pupils had the same options open to them. Pupils who came from a home environment where standard English was spoken were able to choose between the two linguistic forms. However, many more pupils came from homes where standard English was not used and the choices open to these pupils were limited.

Hence, middle class pupils who were more likely to have access to both forms of speech might switch between the two. Conversely, working class children from home environments where patois was routinely used were at a disadvantage in an educational system that depended upon a different linguistic form.

Whilst respondents acknowledged that socialization outside of school fashioned students' interest and proficiency in reading and writing, many simultaneously believed that females were better at some skills while males were better at others because of innate and fundamental differences between the sexes.

For example whereas skills relating to reading and writing were seen as essentially female' skills, analysis and the grasping of concepts were clearly felt to be 'male' skills. The evidence presented in support of this often revolved around students' preferences for particular kinds of tasks. A female biology teacher in an urban boys' school suggested, for example:

"They (boys) would rather do math where there is a concept to grasp. You don't need to explain it in many words and it can be represented in numbers. Boys find it easier to grasp concepts than words."

Similarly, a physics teacher in St Vincent described differences between the work of male and female pupils:

"The girls are more careful in their performance in lab work, in the reporting of results, but when it comes to innovation and design the boys tend to do better."

Any improvement in physics performance of female students was put down to effort rather than aptitude. Hence a male physics teacher at a rural coeducational school suggested:

"Girls make a very great effort in physics. They try very hard and work consistently. The boys don't do this."

Despite the fact that female students may work harder, the following account provided by a Jamaican male physics teacher in a rural coeducational setting demonstrates persistence of the idea that males and female excel in different areas:

"The girls certainly study more than the boys. And they are much better than the boys when it comes to presentation of their results. They write much clearer and the presentation is neater. But when it comes to the concepts then the boys are much better at grasping them than the girls. Usually with a few exceptions the best pupils in the class are the boys. The real difference between them is in the cognitive problem solving. The boys are more cognitive than the girls."

Not only were physics and English felt to encompass different skills, they were seen hierarchically within the curriculum. Many of our science respondents described sciences as "superior to arts subjects". A male physics teacher at an urban coeducational school said that not only did his colleagues in science rate science higher than arts, they encouraged females away from science by saying they would find the math too difficult. In support of his subject, a male physics teacher at an urban all-male school said:

"Well, I encourage my students to do the sciences . . . I always tell my students that the intelligent people do the science subjects."

We found that both male and female respondents perceived differences in the scientific aptitudes of boys and girls. Shepardson and Pizzini (1992) found similar gender bias in teachers' perception of gender aptitude among American teachers, with boys being felt to possess more cognitive intellectual scientific skills than girls.

However, research evidence on difference in gender-related aptitudes is highly inconclusive. Furthermore, there are several factors that influence the direction and performance of gender-related academic interests which are seldom taken into account.

The first is the 'self-fulfilling prophecy' that if girls are expected to do badly in sciences, then this will influence their performance accordingly. Indeed, some of our respondents felt that the performance of female students in science was limited by their expectations. Hence a male physics teacher in a rural coeducational classroom in Jamaica said:

"When I first started teaching very few girls were doing physics, but in the last four years things have changed . . . It has a lot to do with expectation. Girls started doing physics when they expected they could do it. Also I've noticed that since girls have started to do it their performance has changed. Initially they weren't very good, not as good as the boys. But now they are getting better and some are better than the boys."

In some schools we visited, females and males were channelled into particular subject areas which were felt to be gender appropriate. Furthermore, despite protestations from head teachers that there were no gender distinctions in choices open to students, in some schools this was clearly not the case. For example, in some schools technical drawing in the third form was only offered to male students despite the fact that physics teachers told us that technical drawing skills advantaged students taking physics.

"Pupils who do technical drawing have a head start in physics over those who don't. Here unfortunately only the boys do TD. Those girls who chose to do physics start at a disadvantage."

Sex/Gender Identity Development

In this section, data analysis concentrates upon Jamaica because the hard, macho, masculine image informing Caribbean sex/gender identities was most clearly associated, in respondents' accounts, with Jamaica.

"Everything has got to be Jamaican, we are seeing it more and more and it is affecting the young men. The DJs and dancehall coming out of Jamaica – we are getting more and more of it" (Vincentian teacher).

Heads, teachers and guidance counsellors differentiated between the way in which sex/gender identity is constructed for males and females. In the case of females, sex/gender identity was clearly felt to develop through heterosexual relationships which female pupils formed with men outside of school.

Many of the respondents condemned female pupils for relationships that they formed with older men outside of school. Some respondents, like the head teacher from an urban boys' school, described the motivation for selecting older men as mercenary:

"Girls want men to buy them presents and expensive meals . . . some girls go out with really old men."

A female English teacher at an urban coeducational school in Jamaica described how female pupils rejected their male peers for this reason:

"The girls don't want the boys because they don't have the money . . ."

Not all the respondents described the motivations of female pupils as mercenary. The guidance counsellor at a rural coeducational school in Jamaica explained female pupils' sexual rejection of their peers in terms of sexual maturation:

"The girls do mature faster than the boys and say the boys in school are too immature for them even though they are the same age. They go with older men who aren't in school."

Some respondents, like the guidance counsellor at an urban girls' school, felt that it was difficult to judge the behaviour of females by the standards of the school which might run contrary to the expectations of the communities in which they lived:

"You see, if they aren't getting any attention at home they may feel no one loves them. So when someone, a man, shows an interest in them and tells them they are pretty, it is hard to resist. They are under a lot of pressure. It is difficult because although we present a different picture of life in the school, the culture at home is so different and they live it every day."

Other respondents acknowledged how female pupils may be under pressure to assist with the family budget. In this respect, as illustrated in an account provided by the head of an urban girls' school, respondents were ambivalent about the behaviour of females:

"We do get girls who are sponsored by older men. Maybe they will provide for the girl and all her family. It could be a butcher who will provide the family with fresh meat. She will be having a relationship with him. Sometimes I see girls on the bus flirting with the drivers and the conductor. I think they are either having a relationship with the driver or they are about to. They stand behind the drivers and vie for attention. Sometimes competing with each other."

Whether the motivation for involvement with older men was described as biological, mercenary or cultural, respondents clearly condemned girls for the sexual relationships that they formed with men outside of the school. Sexual responsibility was laid squarely at the feet of female pupils. For example, the guidance counsellor cited below locates the responsibility for sexual diseases with girls:

"Because the sexual responsibility is not there in the family with the father, this can lead to problems and we do have problems with sexually transmitted diseases. The girls don't know any better. Even though they are warned it's not until it happens to them that it gets through."

The guidance counsellor at an urban coeducational school acknowledged how issues of responsibility and blame were reinforced by school policies and practices in that a pregnant pupil would be required to leave the school whereas the baby's father could remain at school with no interruption to his education:

"Some of the pupils are sexually active and I try to make sure they are using contraceptives. There is no doubt the girls are at a disadvantage. If a girl at school gets pregnant from a boy at school she really has nothing on that boy. The boy has no problem. The girl will have to leave the school, for maybe a year, or maybe she won't come back. But the boy, he doesn't have to leave. He can stay at school."

In taking responsibility for sexual relationships females are subjected to a double standard which, as the guidance counsellor at the rural coeducational school explained, meant taking the blame:

"Girls can't do what boys do. They think they are probably right, that we will be judgemental. In this respect a girl will feel condemnation."

Sexual rejection by their peers was felt to affect boys' performance in two ways. The first was that in order to attract females, teachers felt, males were pressured into bypassing the education system. The argument in its crudest form goes like this: males understand that females of their own age seek out older men for sexual relationships. They see this as a function of the gifts and money which older men can provide for the females. That is, they interpret the motives of the females as mercenary. In the words of one respondent:

"The boys know this so they want to get money fast"

and another,

"The boys are under pressure so they see a route to get a nice girl."

Based on the extent to which males reject orthodox avenues through education and schooling in order to attract women, females are blamed for the underachievement of male pupils. This position, however, ignores the fact that fourth form males, who were the focus of this research, had access to first, second and third form females. Indeed, some respondents, when talking about relative maturity of boys and girls described how older boys in the school dated younger pupils. Also, the fact that guidance counsellors admitted 'baby fathers' were allowed to remain at school while pregnant females were expelled suggests that the extent of sexual rejection may be less than respondents described.

The second way in which sexual rejection was felt to affect male educational performance related to the development of sex/gender identity. It was clear in respondents' accounts how the sex/gender identity of females was forged through the heterosexual relationships that they formed with older males; relationships for which they were condemned. For males, the development of sex/gender identity was clearly felt to be more problematic. According to teachers, males were sexually rejected by their female peers which meant that development of male sex/gender identity could not be forged in the same way as the females; that is through identification with heterosexual relationships. Conversely, the sex/gender identity for boys emerged, in teachers' accounts, through the rejection of non-heterosexual relationships. The difference between male and female sex/gender identification was captured below by an English teacher at an urban girls' school:

"Girls seem to be more interested in sex at this age whereas I think the boys are more afraid of homosexuality. Jamaican men have to be macho. Homosexuals are run out of the community because of this fear that they have of sexuality."

In the following section we shall see how the construction of an extremely hard, macho and homophobic sex/gender identity has implications for educational efforts and performances.

Masculinities and Homosexuality

In the Caribbean, cultural expectations of male behaviour are informed by an extremely hard, macho, masculine sex/gender identity which is associated with maleness. Anything seen as not male is relegated to the realms of femaleness and devalued as 'nerdish', 'sissyish' and 'effeminate'.

One aspect of this version of masculinity was the rigidity with which it defined appropriate sexual identity and an intolerance of (particularly male) non-heterosexual identities. Many of the respondents expressed homophobic attitudes. Males (both heads and teachers) in particular were quick to assert their opinions about homosexuality and many, like the head of an urban boys' school, made extremely forceful statements such as:

"[My father] thought that homosexuals should be lined up in front of a firing squad. I feel the same way."

Clearly respondents differentiated between homosexual men and lesbians, rarely in fact mentioning the latter except to draw the following kinds of comparisons:

"I don't feel the same about lesbians but it's more difficult to tell with a woman. After all women can hold hands and it's acceptable. But can you imagine if two men walked down the road here holding hands? They would be dead."

One way in which issues of homosexuality materialized in the data was around the recruitment of male teachers, and this has been discussed in a previous section. To reiterate, heads and teachers alike repeatedly voiced the opinion that "there are too many women teachers", "males are sick of seeing women teachers" and "boys need more male teachers as role models". At the same time, however, teaching is not seen as appropriate work for males. In other words, heads simultaneously expressed a concern their male members of staff might not be 'real men' and the very fact they had chosen to teach was seen as just cause for suspicion.

It appeared from the research that to some extent the conventional constructions of Caribbean masculinity and the role of teacher are incompatible. Whereas masculinity is associated with attributes like physical strength and authority, many attributes commonly associated with teaching are traditionally associated with femininity. Because of this, male teachers in the Caribbean cannot be real men and they become the focus of concern and suspicion of their colleagues. However, as our data from St Vincent shows, and as has been discussed earlier, the construction of teaching as a primarily female occupation does not necessarily have to obtain.

Homophobia also has implications for student responses. On the questionnaires, pupils were asked whether they would prefer to be taught in a single sex or a coeducational classroom. Fourteen percent said single sex and 86 percent said coeducational. There was little difference in responses from males and females on this question (50 percent of those who said coeducational were females and 49 percent were males).

Students were then asked to explain the reasons for their response to this question. In Jamaica, 17 percent of males said they preferred coeducation because they did not want to be seen as homosexual. The question was open ended and provoked answers such as "I'm not gay", and 'I don't love a man". None of the female pupils gave homosexuality as a reason for preferring coeducation. The Jamaican responses to this question were more marked than in either of the other two territories. In Barbados 5.6 percent and in St Vincent 2.6 percent of males cited denial of homosexuality as their reason for preferring coeducation over single sex schools. Interestingly, in interviews with 185 Barbadian males (Dann 1987), 69.8 percent said they felt homosexuality was totally wrong and a further 11 percent said it was wrong but inevitable.

Homophobic attitudes have implications for the behaviour of male students. Kimmel (1996) suggests that homophobia, more than simply dread of gay men, symbolizes a male terror of being exposed as something other than heterosexual. This prompts a 'homosocial' enactment which is driven by the fear of being exposed as 'not a real male' by one's peers. This enactment can include classroom behaviour, motivation and educational performance. It can deny legitimacy to anything that is seen as girlish, female or feminine and in doing so dismiss educational efforts as effeminate, nerdish and sissyish.

Respondents repeatedly described an 'anti-academic' ethos of masculinity, which is captured below by a female teacher from St Vincent:

"The boys don't utilize education in the same way. Much of it has to do with image. They don't want to be seen as a nerd and a nerd is someone who works hard at school. They are extremely image conscious. That's not to say the girls aren't. They are sophisticated, stylish and well turned out but the image important to them is not detrimental to their education."

Where males do school work, it is often invisible to the critical gaze of their peers:

"They also prefer to be seen not to work. It's not popular to be male and studious. It's not macho. So some work on the sly. When they do work and apply themselves they will perform very well at tests and in exams and do better than the girls" (Barbadian female teacher).

In schools we found these attitudes reinforced in a number of ways. First, teachers clearly differentiated subject areas along gender lines, and in some cases, curricula channelled males and females into distinctive subject 'choices'. For example, while heads were quick to assure that males and females had equal access to all subjects, this rarely included woodwork or home nutrition which were strictly organized along gender lines. Some respondents told us "the girls aren't encouraged to go into the workshops" and asked, "Well why would a boy want to do food and nutrition?" Subjects like technical drawing were felt to be 'inappropriate' for female pupils, despite the fact that the skills acquired in technical drawing advantaged students entering physics. Furthermore, certain skills were described by respondents as more feminine than others. English language and literature in particular clearly fell into this category. Consequently reading and writing were dismissed by male students as girlish, nerdish and effeminate.

Certainly some of the respondents were aware of the debilitating effects of these attitudes on the performance of males in other subjects. For example, science teachers expressed great concern about the inability of male students to present their work in acceptable English; a shortcoming for which they are penalized in examinations.

Second, teachers held clear expectations of gender-appropriate behaviour in the classroom. Male students were openly acknowledged as "rougher" and "more boisterous" than their female peers. Males who disregarded these expectations were policed both by peers and in some cases, teachers who labelled them derogatively and admonished what was described as "sissyish behaviour of boys".

In many respects, gendered responses were most noticeable in Jamaica. Respondents clearly identified Jamaica as the 'home' or 'leader' of the 'macho West Indian male' image. Respondents from both Barbados and St Vincent talked about how adolescent males were increasingly influenced by the music and dancehall scene emanating from Jamaica in this respect:

"Everything has to be Jamaican. Videos, the music and DJs and dancehall. It's becoming more and more popular and it's definitely having an effect on our young males" (Vincentian female teacher).

To reiterate, many respondents felt that behaviour and participation in class work of male students was influenced by the presence of female students. Heads, teachers and counsellors stressed how male students were unwilling to be 'shown up' or 'wrong' in front of female peers. Respondents also felt that male students were unwilling to compete with female students due to fear of failure. This fear had, according to teachers, implications for the level of class participation in which male students were prepared to engage.

This account distances itself from explanations that locate male responses solely in the context of female audiences. On the contrary, the study suggested that the audience for whom 'masculinities' were enacted was primarily male. For example, the hard, macho, masculine sex/gender identity that informed behaviour in the coeducational classrooms, was also apparent in the male single sex schools. In other words, there was no evidence in the study to suggest that males are less concerned about being 'shown up' in front of other males than they are concerned about being 'shown up' in front of females.

It was equally interesting how female teachers in the male schools were no less adamant than those in coeducational schools about their preference for teaching male students. Teachers in the single sex setting felt, like their coeducation colleagues, that male students were "more resilient", "straightforward" and, as a result, "easier to teach than females". This even held true for female teachers who had no experience of teaching females.

To this extent, the data endorses the position of Kimmel (1996) who argues that masculinity is the renunciation of femininity or the fear of being seen as sensitive, fragile or frail by male peers. If maleness or manhood is primarily demonstrated through the approval and endorsement of other men then its underlying concern derives from the fear of being exposed or unmasked as a fraud by other males. The hard, macho masculine behaviour observed in the Caribbean classroom represents what Kimmel describes as a homosocial enactment which masks the concern of males that they may not measure up among their peers (Kaufman 1996). As Pleck (1989) argues, this horror of being exposed, unmasked and emasculated is accompanied by stress and strain which arises due to fear of failure. This fear of failure, or inability to convince, involves the constant public rejection or negation of anything that is identified as unmasculine.

Concluding Discussion

Our research findings have suggested that the hard macho, male image with which young Caribbean males identify runs counter to their educational interests. However, it is equally obvious that not all young males fail in school. This raises the question, which young men fail and which succeed in school?

Many of our respondents felt that the most problematic period for male achievement was in the fourth and fifth forms. This was summed up below by a female teacher in Jamaica and was reinforced by many heads, teachers and counsellors who took part in the study:

"When they get into the sixth form everything is different. It's not the same. They know they are there to work and they really apply themselves."

It was as if sixth form culture sanctioned educational effort and achievement in a way that the culture of previous forms did not. Furthermore, this reinforced the opinion of many of the respondents who clearly felt that once male pupils start striving to achieve then they achieved equally to their female peers. However, this still begs the question, why do some males enter the sixth form while others leave school?

The study has stressed that schools do not exist in a vacuum and indeed they cannot 'compensate for society'. Not all pupils enter the education system equally equipped to compete. Some pupils will be advantaged as a result of their home experiences but others may find that their home experiences are not considered legitimate at school. This point was raised in a previous discussion in regard to the use of patois. Whereas some (middle class) pupils will have access to both standard English and patois and are able to switch between the two, other less advantaged pupils will be handicapped in that the linguistic form which they routinely use at home is dismissed as inappropriate by the school.

The above example is offered as just one way in which the social class background of pupils may assist or militate against educational success. It is a particularly poignant example in that it highlights the fact that some pupils are in a position to make choices while others are not.

The male culture of the school embraces a very hard and anti-education image with which male pupils identify. It is arguable, however, that whereas middle class pupils are equipped with the necessary resources to opt for an alternative masculine identity (which does not demean educational efforts or rewards), less advantaged pupils do not have the same options. By the end of the fifth form, the educational fates of pupils are all but sealed in cases where resources are unavailable. However, middle class pupils have access to those resources that foster educational success.

Middle class pupils, for example, are more likely to come from families where educational success is the norm, where higher education is expected and where the provision of facilities (books, materials and a place to study) are commonplace. These pupils may educationally succeed despite earlier identification with an anti-education school culture. Male culture in the sixth form is far removed from the anti-education culture of previous forms and provides an environment where, for those male pupils who have not left school, education is no longer equated with being nerdish, sissish or effeminate.

Caribbean females are doing better than they used to and are outperforming their male peers in some subject areas. However, in focusing on male underachievement we must not lose sight of the fact that females are still channelled into 'traditional' (lower status) academic areas and face discrimination when they enter the occupational arena upon leaving school.

Where educational expectations and occupational realities are synchronized, then education can be used effectively to an end. Unfortunately, changing global economies have implications for education systems that are not equipped with the resources to respond appropriately. If male pupils understand that education will not guarantee the promised rewards of social engineering then we should not be surprised when, as our findings suggest, the value of education has become, in their eyes, demeaned.

However, this is not a sufficient explanation for the lack of motivation and educational effort expended by boys. Girls face lower glass ceilings in the occupational structure than boys and yet educationally they continue to both strive and achieve.

Nor is it appropriate to allow educators to take full responsibility for male underachievement. The majority of the teachers who participated in the study demonstrated a level of commitment and dedication to their role far exceeding the level of social and economic recognition which they receive for their efforts.

The main finding of the study is that the current construction of male sex gender identity in the Caribbean has implications for educational underachievement of Caribbean males. This theme ran throughout the analysis, emerging from data collected in Jamaica, Barbados, and St Vincent and the Grenadines. At the same time, data reflected some differences in the way in which the problem of male underachievement is perceived in the three territories which participated in the research. The findings suggest these are largely differences in degree, which at least partly stem from differences in the organization of education systems and institutions in the respective countries.

Male sex/gender identity currently informing educational attitudes, motivations and performances is extremely homophobic. It is a construction that emerges in fierce opposition to and rejection of non-heterosexual identities. In distancing itself from marginal non-heterosexual identities it openly rejects anything construed as remotely female, feminine or effeminate. Unfortunately, through this process of rejection, education has become equated with the 'female' side of the competing dichotomies female/academic versus male/non-academic. Because of this educational motivation, efforts and achievements are dismissed by many boys as effeminate, sissyish and nerdish.

Whilst educationalists appear to recognize that male gender identity as it is currently constructed runs contrary to the academic ethos of education, it is encouraged in schools in several ways. Pupils are still encouraged and channelled into gender-appropriate subject areas. Certain subjects are felt to be more suitable for girls and others more suitable for boys. Furthermore, there are widespread assumptions among educators that girls and boys have innate aptitudes which render particular subjects more suited to them. Whereas females are felt to be good at reading and writing, males are felt to excel in higher status skills like cognitive problem solving. This fuels the understanding that males are more suited to higher status science subjects like physics while females excel in English. Even where females outperform males in science subjects, this is often put down to sheer determination and slog rather than ability.

The results of this study suggest that encouragement (or lack of it) and subject engineering continue to propel pupils into gender-related areas which are then interpreted as 'natural' choices. Furthermore, teachers' expectations about gender-appropriate choices contradict their understanding about gender socialization patterns outside of school. It is widely understood, for example, how females develop responsibility (through domestic tasks) and acquire home-based activities, such as reading. In combination these factors prepare girls for the educational regime they meet at school. Conversely, boys are freed from domestic responsibilities endured by their sisters. The extra-school pursuits in which boys participate are street rather than home-based. Teachers do recognize that boys tend not to read as much as girls and also feel that this seriously handicaps their educational outcomes, not only in English but across all subjects.

High school entrance examinations (and the preceding syllabuses) do not require boys to develop the type of skills (reading and writing) that they clearly lack. Therefore, what they do not acquire at home they are ill prepared for by education prior to starting high school. This puts males at a further disadvantage.

Teachers are clearly aware of gender-distinct responses in classroom behaviour, many of which they tend to attribute to 'natural' or 'innate' biological difference. Teachers expect boys and girls to behave differently in the classroom. They expect males to be more boisterous, noisy and disruptive, and they expect girls to be more 'manageable'. Furthermore, boys are not expected to display any 'sensitive' tendencies and are policed by both peers and staff in this respect.

The findings suggest that some gender-related responses have less to do with natural differences than they do with cultural expectations about how Caribbean males and females are supposed to respond. These expectations are translated into pedagogical relationships and have become part of routine teacher/pupil interaction. Teacher expectations of gender responses have implications for educational performances, and one area where this was particularly noticeable in the research related to verbal discipline in the classroom.

Sarcasm and ridicule are two strategies of verbal discipline used routinely by some (particularly untrained and inexperienced teachers) in the classroom. Whereas female pupils respond adversely to these discipline strategies by "sulking," "bearing grudges" and "giving looks", to males it's like "water off a duck's back". Many female teachers feel because of this that males are easier to teach and hence prefer to teach boys.

The research findings suggest that males do not openly respond adversely to verbal disciplining because they are not expected, inside or outside school, to be 'soft' or 'sensitive'. That males do not respond openly to such strategies does not necessarily mean that they are any less sensitive, but rather they are conforming to the stereotypical way in which males are expected to respond.

While male teachers appear to largely avoid adverse responses from female pupils by treating them differently from their male peers, both male and female teachers expect male pupils to withstand harsher regimes. Given that sarcasm and ridicule as disciplining strategies are detrimental to educational outcomes, expectations about males may be exacerbating their educational underperformance in this respect.

Underachievement of males has fuelled the case for single sex education in the Caribbean. Although the case for single sex education for males in particular was argued at all three research sites, it was most forcibly put in Barbados, where sixteen years ago single sex schools were amalgamated to become coeducational institutions. After sixteen years' experience of collocation, many educators argue males do better where they are largely taught (a) by men (b) in all-male single sex classrooms. This study challenges both these assumptions, supporting previous research findings that emphasize the importance of expectations which participants bring with them to any educational innovation.

Furthermore, teaching in the Caribbean is largely seen as a female occupation because (a) it is poorly paid and (b) it encompasses particular skills, such as emotional support and caring, which have traditionally been seen as 'women's work'. Because teaching in some Caribbean territories is not seen as a masculine, male or macho occupation, male teachers are sometimes the target of suspicion among colleagues. If, as at present, male teachers in the Caribbean cannot currently qualify as 'real men' then it is difficult to conceive how they can usefully become role models for male pupils.

The findings suggest that teaching does not necessarily have to be seen as women's work. The organization of the occupation along professional lines, with the provision of education and training opportunities, career paths and appropriate remuneration packages, would make teaching an attractive occupational choice for both men and women. In St Vincent, where in the past teaching has created opportunities for further education and training plus career advancement in the civil service, more males are found in teaching, particularly in their early career stages.

Males who do teach tend to be located in 'traditional' male subject areas, like math and physics, which further perpetuates stereotypical conceptions of gender-appropriate subjects, skills and aptitudes. Furthermore, some male teachers refuse to perform tasks (such as the correction of English grammar) because they see it as 'women's' domain.

Claims that the presence of female pupils in classrooms adversely affects educational performances of males should be treated with caution. The hard, macho, masculine behaviour, which runs contrary to educational requirements, was no less evident in male single sex schools in the study than coeducational schools. Conversely, the data suggest that demonstrations of masculinity may mainly target male audiences. If this is so then the exclusive company of male pupils may exacerbate the rejection of education by males as sissyish, nerdish and effeminate.

The study suggests that selection policies that discriminate against females to increase male entry into high school have implications for male under performance. While some educators defend such policies on the grounds that females mature faster than boys, others are equally aware that allowing less able males into high school exacerbates the problems which male pupils already face. Not only do the female pupils seem more mature but they have, as a group, educationally outclassed their male peers. Male pupils are aware of this and the knowledge that they are starting high school at a (double) disadvantage ill prepares them psychologically for educational success.

British research highlights a mismatch in the masculinized orientation of education (which promotes qualities like competitiveness and differentiation) and the way in which certain masculinities are valued (Weekes et al. 1996). This mismatch is evident in our Caribbean data which suggest that Caribbean masculinity informing classroom responses is at variance with the requirements of the education system. The mismatch was most noticeable in Jamaica where, arguably, the hard, macho, male image is most celebrated in popular culture.

Furthermore, Caribbean systems of education themselves have a precarious relationship with (in an age of structural adjustment) the changing socioeconomic and political climates of developing countries. Among other changes, the growing economic independence of Caribbean females has rendered the core claims to Caribbean masculinity (control over women and their economic subordination within the family) both inappropriate and unrealizable. This is certainly an area in which further research would be welcomed.

Appendix 1

Policy Options and Practical Solutions

The preceding sections have identified several ways in which educators interpret and reinforce gender-distinct responses in the classroom. The research suggests ways in which these responses reflect wider cultural expectations about the way we feel males and females should behave under the guise of being informed by natural differences between males and females.

The report further suggests that some gender-distinct responses which are seen as natural and necessary run counter to the academic aims of education. In this research we have explored the implications of some of these responses for the educational motivation and performance of Caribbean males.

When addressing male underachievement, the report stresses that measures that target one gender (particularly at the expense of the other) will not work. Although Caribbean girls are doing better than they used to and are outperforming boys in some subject areas, girls are still channelled into 'traditional' (lower status) academic areas and face discrimination when they enter the occupational arena upon leaving school. Issues of underachievement must be tackled holistically with a view to making educational opportunities and outcomes more equal for both girls and boys.

Furthermore, the research stresses that teachers should not be held fully accountable for male underachievement. The majority of the teachers who participated in the study demonstrated a level of commitment and dedication to their role far exceeding the level of social and economic recognition that they receive for their efforts.

The report targets several areas for change. It recommends practical action by educators which will alter aspects of teacher/pupil interaction and attention to some areas of educational policy that reinforce gender responses. These recommendations emerged from the research findings and through feedback on these findings from educators and policy makers.

Education Policy

1. At present, the disproportionately low numbers of males in teaching is a source of concern. The organization of the occupation along professional lines with the provision of education and training opportunities, career paths and appropriate remuneration packages would make teaching an attractive occupational choice for both men and women.
2. Teacher recruitment should target both male and female role models who present appropriate positive and non-sexist approaches to education.
3. All teachers, irrespective of higher educational qualifications, should hold an appropriate teacher training qualification.
4. All educational innovation and change should follow adequate preparation for change in order to avoid self-fulfilling expectations and uninformed prejudices of participants.
5. Gender differences often reflect cultural biases and should not be exaggerated and used as the basis for policy decisions.
6. Education policies that discriminate against either gender tackle only the symptoms of underlying problems (such as disproportionate gender entry into high schools) and not the root causes.
7. Selection procedures (and their preceding syllabuses) must target areas of weakness currently demonstrated by both genders respectively.
8. The effectiveness of government funding in education depends as much upon how it is targeted as the amount allocated. Two areas identified as those most in need of input are primary levels of education and the less advantaged sectors of secondary education.

Educators

1. Gender should not be used as the factor that dictates the opportunity to pursue any curriculum choice.
2. Guidance on subject choice should not propel either sex into what are currently seen as gender-appropriate subjects.
3. Pupil expectations of their aptitude and abilities in what are currently seen as gender-appropriate subjects should be addressed.
4. Special critical attention should be directed towards the syllabus and teaching method of any subject which has come to be associated with one gender in particular.
5. Educators should be sensitive to the type of verbal disciplinary strategies that they use. At present, some (particularly untrained and inexperienced teachers) are unaware of the sensitivity of both male and female pupils. Insensitive strategies of verbal discipline (sarcasm and ridicule) are detrimental to the educational performances of all pupils.
6. Gender responses in the classroom often reflect cultural expectations about gender differences. These are translated into classroom practices and are evident in routine teacher pupil interaction. It is important, therefore, that a positive and reciprocal learning relationship should be encouraged and fostered between home and school.

Appendix 2

Summary of the Research Findings

Through a qualitative appraisal of classroom practices the study set out to explore aspects of gender responses in high school education which have implications for the educational performances of Caribbean males.

Concern with male educational achievement reflects a wider global concern about the position of males (and particularly black males) in society who are increasingly being depicted in both popular culture and social science as 'marginalized', 'in crisis' and 'at risk'.

The danger of these depictions is not that black males are not undoubtedly facing a broad array of social and economic problems but that these issues are being taken out of context. Black males do not exist in isolation, many belong to families, alongside women, live in communities and are members of complex societies.

The research starts from the premise that the issues that confront males acquire meaning and significance in the wider contexts in which they occur and in relation to others with whom they interact.

Because of this, the study focuses upon educational motivations and performances by examining them at both the level of classroom interaction and as a reflection of the demands and expectations of the wider culture in which they are embedded.

Main Findings

1. The extremely hard macho, male image of Caribbean men with which young Caribbean males seek to identify runs contrary to the academic ethos of education and militates against their educational motivation and performance.
2. Male gender identity as it is currently constructed has implications for classroom behaviour, educational motivation, participation in classes and educational performance.

3. Although educationalists recognize how male gender identity as it is currently constructed runs contrary to the ethos of schooling, it is nevertheless encouraged in schools in a number of ways.
4. Pupils are still channelled into what are seen as gender-appropriate subject areas.
5. Pupils' expectations that they are more suited to these gender-appropriate subjects are encouraged and reinforced by some educationalists.
6. Performance in English, which is largely rejected as a 'female subject' by male pupils, is critical for educational performance across all subjects.
7. Teachers attribute some gender-differentiated classroom behaviour to immutable differences between males and females and fail to recognize the extent to which gender responses reflect cultural attitudes and expectations about how males and females are supposed to behave. Furthermore, these differences have been used as the basis of educational selection policies which discriminate against female entry into high school.
8. The use of educationally harmful strategies of verbal disciplining, such as sarcasm and ridicule, is justified by the belief of many (untrained inexperienced) teachers that boys are more resilient and less sensitive than females.
9. The very different home socialization experiences of male and female pupils means that they are not equally equipped to cope with the exigencies of schooling.
10. The high ratio of female to male teachers contributes to the notion that education has become 'feminized'. It is difficult to attract male teachers into the profession because of poor remuneration and because teaching is currently seen as 'women's work'.

Recommendations: Policy Initiatives

1. The occupation of teaching should be made a more attractive career option for both males and females. As is the case with other professions, like medicine and law, teaching should provide education and training opportunities, structured career paths and appropriate remuneration packages.
2. Teacher recruitment should target both male and female role models who present appropriate positive and non-sexist approaches to education.
3. All teachers, irrespective of higher educational qualifications, should hold an appropriate teacher training qualification. Just as we do not expect to be operated on by untrained doctors, we should not expect children to be taught by unqualified teachers.
4. All educational innovation and change should follow adequate preparation for change in order to avoid self-fulfilling expectations and uninformed prejudices of participants.
5. Gender differences often reflect cultural biases and should not be exaggerated and used as the basis for policy decisions.
6. Selection procedures (and their preceding syllabuses) must target areas of weakness currently demonstrated by both genders respectively.
7. The effectiveness of government funding in education depends as much upon how it is targeted as the amount allocated. Two areas identified as those most in need of input are primary levels of education and the less advantaged sectors of secondary education.

Recommendations: Inside Schools

1. Gender should not be used as the factor that dictates the opportunity to pursue any curriculum choice.
2. Guidance on subject choice should not propel either sex into what are currently seen as gender-appropriate subjects.

3. Pupil expectations of their aptitude and abilities in what are currently seen as gender-appropriate subjects should be addressed.
4. Special critical attention should be directed towards the syllabus and teaching method of any subject that has come to be associated with one gender in particular.
5. Educators should be sensitive to the type of verbal disciplinary strategies that they use.
6. Gender responses in the classroom often reflect cultural expectations about gender differences. It is important, therefore, that a positive and reciprocal learning relationship should be encouraged and fostered between home and school.

Bibliography

Atkinson, P. 1979. "Research Design in Ethnography." *The Open University Research Methods in Education and the Social Sciences* 5. Keynes: Open University Press.

Ayodike, T. 1989. "Images of Women in Selected CXC Literature." Paper presented at Gender and Education, Third Disciplinary Seminar, Kingston, Jamaica.

Barrow, C. 1988. "Anthropology, the Family and Women in the Caribbean." In *Gender in Caribbean Development*, edited by P. Mohammed and C. Shepherd. Mona, Jamaica: University of the West Indies Women and Development Project.

Beckles, H. 1996. "Black Masculinity in Caribbean Slavery." Paper presented at the conference, The Construction of Caribbean Masculinity: Towards a Research Agenda, University of the West Indies, St Augustine, Trinidad.

Bernard, J. 1982. *The Future of Marriage*. New Haven: Yale University Press.

Bernstein, B. 1977. *Class Codes and Control: Towards a Theory of Educational Transmission*. London: Routledge and Kegan Paul.

Brown, J., and B. Chevannes. 1995. "Findings of the Gender Socialization Project." Paper presented at the annual UNICEF Global Seminar, Achieving Gender Equality in Families: The Roles of Males, Caribbean Child Development Centre, University of the West Indies, Mona, Jamaica.

Burgess, R.G. 1984. *In The Field: An Introduction to Field Research*. London: Allen and Unwin.

Carrington, H. 1993. "Coeducation and Academic Achievement in Barbados." MA thesis, University of the West Indies, Cave Hill, Barbados.

Connell, R. 1985. *Teachers' Work*. London: Allen and Unwin.

Connell, R.W. 1995. *Masculinities*. Cambridge, Mass.: Polity Press.

Cuffie, J. 1989. "Gender and Subject Choice in Secondary School." Paper presented at Gender and Education, Third Disciplinary Seminar, Kingston, Jamaica.

Dale, R. 1962. "Coeducation: A Critical Analysis of Research on Effects of Coeducation on Academic Attainment in Grammar Schools." *Educational Research* 4: 207–15.

Dann, G. 1987. *The Barbadian Male*. London: Macmillan Caribbean.

De Marris, A., and G.L. Greif. 1992. "The Relationship Between Family Structure and Parent Child Relationship Problems in Single Father Households." *Journal of Divorce and Remarriage* 18, nos. 1–2: 55–77.

Denzin, N. 1978. *The Research Act: A Theoretical Introduction to Sociological Methods*. New York: McGraw-Hill.

Department of Education. 1987a. *Minorities in Higher Education: 6th Annual Report*. Kingston, Jamaica: Ministry of Education.

Department of Education. 1987b. *High School Enrolment*. Kingston, Jamaica: Ministry of Education.

Dill, B. 1987. "The Dialectics of Black Womanhood." In *Feminism and Methodology*, edited by S. Harding. Indianapolis: Indiana University Press.

Drayton, K. 1991. *Gender Bias in Education*. WAND Occasional Papers no. 2/91. St Michael, Barbados: Women and Development Unit, University of the West Indies.

Elliot, V. 1995. "Black Schoolboys 'Need Male Role Model'." *Sunday Telegraph*, 10 September.

Epstein, C. 1993. "Positive Effects of the Multiple Negative." In *Changing Women in a Changing Society*, edited by J. Huber. Chicago: University of Chicago Press.

Furlong, V. 1977. "Anancy Goes to School: A Case Study of Pupils' Knowledge about Their Teachers." In *School Experience*, edited by P. Woods and M. Hammersley. London: Croom Helm.

Galwey, J. 1970. "Classroom Discipline: What Pupils Think." *Comprehensive Education* 14: 24–25.

Gaskell, J.H. 1960. "Children and Punishment: A Scottish Attitude Survey." *Research Review* 3: 12–16.

Glaser, B., and A. Strauss. 1967. *The Discovery of Grounded Theory for Qualitative Research*. Chicago: Aldine.

Goffman, E. 1968. *Asylums: Essays on the Social Situation of Mental Patients and Other Inmates*. Harmondsworth: Pelican.

Gordon, D. 1986. "Occupational Segregation and Inter-generational Mobility in Jamaica." In *Sociological Research Unit Working Paper*. Cardiff: College of Cardiff, University of Wales.

Gordon, D. 1989. "Class Status and Social Mobility in Jamaica." In *Population, Mobility and Development Studies*. Mona, Jamaica: Institute of Social and Economic Research.

Hammersley, H. 1984. "The Researcher Exposed: A Natural History." In *The Research Process in Educational Settings: Ten Case Studies*, edited by R.G. Burgess. London: Falmer Press.

Hammersley, M., and P. Atkinson. 1983. *Ethnography: Principles In Practice*. London: Tavistock.

Hamilton, M. 1981. "The Prediction of Academic Success: An Interim Report." *Caribbean Journal of Education* 8: 43–58.

Handra, S. 1994. "The Determinants of Teenage Schooling in Jamaica: Rich vs Poor, Females vs Males." Typescript, University of the West Indies, Mona, Jamaica.

Haywood, C., and M. Mac An Ghaill. 1996. "Schooling Masculinities." In *Understanding Masculinities*, edited by M. Mac An Ghaill. Buckingham: Open University Press.

Herzog, E., and C. Sudia. 1971. "Children in Fatherless Families." In *Review of Child Development Research* 3B, edited by H. Cadwell and H. Ricciult. Chicago: University of Chicago Press.

Honigmann, J.J. 1982. "Sampling in Ethnographic Fieldwork." In *Field Research: A Source Book and Field Manual*, edited by R.G. Burgess. London: Allen and Unwin.

Johnson, U. 1996. "The Reconstruction of Masculinity: Breaking the Link Between Maleness and Violence." Paper presented at the conference, The Construction of Caribbean Masculinity: Towards a Research Agenda, University of the West Indies, St Augustine, Trinidad.

Kaufman, M. 1996. "A Theoretical Framework for the Study of Men and Masculinities." Paper presented at the conference, The Construction of Caribbean Masculinity: Towards a Research Agenda, University of the West Indies, St Augustine, Trinidad.

Kimmel, M. 1996. "Masculinity as Homophobia: Fear, Shame and Silence in the Construction of Gender Identity." Paper presented at the conference, The Construction of Caribbean Masculinity: Towards a Research Agenda, University of the West Indies, St Augustine, Trinidad.

Klein, S., ed. 1985. *Handbook for Achieving Sex Equity Through Education*. Baltimore: Johns Hopkins University Press.

Laureau, A. 1992. "Gender Differences in Parent Involvement in Schooling." In *Education and Gender Equality*, edited by J. Wrigley. London: Falmer Press.

Lee, V.E., and A.S. Bryck. 1988. "Effects of Single Sex Schools on Student Achievement and Attitudes." *Journal of Educational Psychology* 78: 381–95.

Leo-Rhynie, E. 1989. "Gender Issues in Secondary School Placement." Paper presented at Gender and Education, Third Disciplinary Seminar, Kingston, Jamaica.

Leo-Rhynie, E. 1992. "Women and Development Studies: Moving From the Periphery." Women and Development Studies Tenth Anniversary Symposium, University of the West Indies, Mona, Jamaica.

Lewis, L. 1996. "Caribbean Masculinity at the Fin De Siecle." Paper presented at the conference, The Construction of Caribbean Masculinity: Towards a Research Agenda, University of the West Indies, St Augustine, Trinidad.

Lewis, R., and M. Lovegrove. 1987. "The Teacher as Disciplinarian: How Do Students Feel?" *Australian Journal of Education* 31: 173–86.

MacMillan, V. 1981. "Academic Motivation of Adolescent Jamaican Girls in Selected Single Sex and Coeducational High Schools." MA thesis, University of the West Indies, Mona, Jamaica.

Mac An Ghaill, M. 1994. *The Making of Men*. Buckingham: Open University Press.

Mickelson, R.A. 1992. "Why Does Jane Read and Write So Well? The Anomaly of Women's Achievement." In *Education and Gender Equality*, edited by J. Wrigley. London: Falmer Press.

Miller, E. 1986. *Marginalization of the Black Male*. Mona, Jamaica: Institute of Social and Economic Research.

Miller, E. 1989. "Gender Composition of the Primary School Teaching Force: A Result of Personal Choice?" Paper presented at Gender and Education, Third Disciplinary Seminar, Kingston, Jamaica.

Miller, E. 1991. *Men at Risk*. Kingston, Jamaica: Jamaica Publishing House.

Mirza, H. 1992. *Young Female and Black*. London: Routledge.

Mohammed, P. 1996. "Unmasking Masculinity and Deconstructing Patriarchy: Problems and Possibilities Within Feminist Epistemology." Paper presented at the conference, The Construction of Caribbean Masculinity: Towards a Research Agenda, University of the West Indies, St Augustine, Trinidad.

Noguera, P. 1996. "The Crisis of the Black Male in Comparative Perspective." Paper presented at the conference, The Construction of Caribbean Masculinity: Towards a Research Agenda, University of the West Indies, St Augustine, Trinidad.

Oakley, A. 1981. "Interviewing Women." In *Doing Feminist Research,* edited by H. Roberts. London: Routledge.

Ogbu, J.U. 1978. *Minority Education and Caste.* New York: Academic Press.

Olesen, V.W., and E. Whittaker. 1968. "Critical Notes on Sociological Studies of Professional Socialization." In *Social Studies 2: Professional Socialization,* edited by A. Jackson. Cambridge: Cambridge University Press.

Parry, O. 1990. "Fitting in with the Setting: A Problem of Adjustment for Both Students and the Researcher." *Sociology* 24, no. 3: 417–30.

Parry, O. 1992. "Making Sense of the Research Setting and Making the Research Setting Make Sense." In *Studies in Qualitative Education* 3, edited by R. Burgess. London: JAI Press.

Parry, O. 1995. "What's Sex Got to Do with It?: Odette Parry Explores Why Some West Indian Boys in Jamaica Fail in School and Explodes the Myth That It's All the Girls' Fault." *Guardian,* Education Supplement, 5 September.

Parry, O. 1996. "Equality, Gender and the Caribbean Classroom." *Twenty-first Century Policy Review Special Issue: Institutional Development in the Caribbean: Acting Upon Changing Structures* 3, no. 12: 178–97.

Parry, O. 1997. "Schooling Is Fooling: Why Do Jamaican Boys Underachieve in School?" *Gender and Education* 9, no. 2: 223–31.

Payne, M. 1988. "Discipline and Punishment in Barbadian Secondary Schools: The Student's Perspective." In *Faculty of Education Occasional Paper* 1. Cave Hill, Barbados: Faculty of Education, University of the West Indies.

Pleck, J.A. 1989. "Prisoners of Manliness." In *Men's Lives,* edited by M. Kimmel and M. Messner. New York: Macmillan.

Raven, J. 1976. "A Survey of Attitudes of Post Primary Teachers and Pupils." In *Pupil Motivation and Values* 3, Dublin: Irish Association for Curriculum Development.

Ritchie, J., and J. Ritchie. 1981. *Spare the Rod.* Sydney: Allen and Unwin.

Riordan, C. 1985. "Public and Catholic Schooling: The Effects of Gender Context Policy." *American Journal of Education* 5: 581–640.

Roth, J. 1962. "Comments on Secret Observation." *Social Problems* 3: 91–99.

Salter, V. 1989. "Factors Affecting Females Choice of Non-Traditional Careers in Jamaica." Paper presented at Caribbean Studies Association fourteenth annual conference, Bridgetown, Barbados.

Schiefelbein, E., and S. Peruzzi. 1991. "Education Opportunities for Women: The Case of Latin America and the Caribbean." *OREALC Bulletin: Major Projects in the Field of Education in Latin America and the Caribbean* 24.

Shepardson, D.P., and E.L. Pizzini. 1992. "Gender, Achievement and Perception Toward Science Activities." *School Science and Mathematics* 94, 188–93.

Spindler, G. 1982. *Doing the Ethnography of Schooling: Anthropology in Action.* New York: Holt, Rhinehart and Winston.

Spradley, J.P. 1980. *Participant Observation.* New York: Holt, Rhinehart and Winston.

Stack, C. 1974. *All Our Kin.* New York: Harper Touchstone.

Stanworth, M. 1983. *Gender and Schooling: Study of Social Divisions in the Classroom.* London: Hutchinson.

Stockard, J. 1985. "Education and Gender Equality: A Critical View." In *Research in Sociology of Education and Socialization* 5, edited by R. Burgess. London: JAI Press.

Stockard, J., and J.W. Wood. 1984. "The Myth of Female Underachievement: A Re-examination of Sex Differences in Academic Underachievement." *American Educational Research Journal* 21, no. 40: 825–38.

Sutton, C., and S. Makiesky-Barrow. 1977. "Social Inequality and Sexual Status in Barbados." In *Sexual Stratification: A Cross-Cultural View,* edited by A. Schlegel. New York: Columbia University Press.

Walford, G. 1983. "Girls in Boys' Public Schools: A Prelude to Further British Research." *Journal of Sociology of Education* 4: 39–54.

Watts, M. 1989. "The Study of Literature in School Is Mostly for Girls: Some Implications for Curriculum Goals, Implementation and Research." Paper presented at Gender and Education, Third Disciplinary Seminar, Kingston, Jamaica.

Weekes, D., et al. 1996. "Masculinized Discourses Within Education and the Construction of Black Male Identities Amongst African Caribbean Youth." Paper presented at the annual BSA conference, University of Reading.

Willis, P. 1977. *Learning to Labour: How Working Class Kids Get Working Class Jobs.* Aldershot: Saxon House.

Wilson, F.C. 1982. "A Look at Corporeal Punishment and Some of the Implications of its Use." *Child Abuse and Neglect* 6: 155–64.

Whitely, P. 1994. "Equal Opportunity? Gender and Participation in Science Education in Jamaica." Unpublished working paper, Department of Education, University of the West Indies, Mona, Jamaica.

Woods, P. 1975. "Showing Them up in Secondary School." In *Frontiers of Classroom Research,* edited by G. Chanan and S. Delamont. Windsor: National Foundation For Educational Research.

Woods, P. 1986. *Inside Schools: Ethnography in Educational Research.* London: Routledge and Kegan Paul.

World Bank. 1993. *Access Quality and Efficiency in Education.* World Bank Country Study. Washington, DC: World Bank.

www.ingramcontent.com/pod-product-compliance
Lightning Source LLC
Chambersburg PA
CBHW022017160426
43197CB00007B/461